Light from the East

Light from the East

A Symposium on the Oriental Orthodox and Assyrian Churches

Compiled and edited by
The Rt Rev Henry Hill

Anglican Book Centre
Toronto, Canada

1988
Anglican Book Centre
600 Jarvis Street
Toronto, Ontario
Canada M4Y 2J6

Typesetting by Jay Tee Graphics Ltd.

Canadian Cataloguing in Publication Data

Main entry under title:

Light from the East

ISBN 0-919891-90-X

1. Oriental Orthodox churches. 2. Oriental Orthodox churches – History. 3. Nestorian Church. 4. Nestorian Church – History. I. Hill, Henry G.

BX106.2.L53 1988   281'.5   C88-094154-5

Dedication

This symposium is a result of the reawakening of contact between the Anglican communion and the Oriental Orthodox churches and the Assyrian Church of the East. It is dedicated to the Most Reverend Robert Runcie and the Most Reverend Edward Scott whose blessing and encouragement made that reawakening possible.

Contents

Introduction

Henry Hill

The four historic Oriental Orthodox churches are national churches in the Middle East and South India: the Armenian Apostolic in Soviet Armenia and Lebanon; the Coptic Orthodox of Egypt; the Ethiopian Orthodox; and the Syrian Orthodox churches comprising the see of Antioch and the Syrian Thomas Christians of South India. These churches are a family; but each has a unique story to tell, and no general description will cover all of them. All were separated from the Great Church, some as early as the Fourth Ecumenical Council of Chalcedon, AD 451, which defined Orthodox Christology of the two natures, human and divine, in the person of Christ. Henceforth considered Monophysite heretics, these Orthodox churches lived their lives in obscurity, producing their saints, confessors, and martyrs. In later centuries, under the yoke of Islamic and Mongol invasions, they were largely ignored by Roman Catholic and Byzantine Christianity until "rediscovered" between the sixteenth and eighteenth centuries by European Catholic missionaries who sought to unite them to the papacy. In the nineteenth century Protestant missionaries built hospitals, colleges, and schools in an attempt to win the Oriental Orthodox for the churches of the Reformation.

The Anglican relationship to these churches is somewhat different; in friendships extending over more than a century, we have tried to support, rather than to absorb them.

The fifth church, the Catholic Assyrian Church of the East, broke its official relationship with the churches to the west of it at the Council of Ephesus, AD 431, resulting in the Nestorian schism. In later centuries, Nestorian monks carried on a magnificent missionary enterprise as far as India and China, using the Persian Empire as its base. Once numbering millions of faithful, the Assyrian church is now, through persecution, reduced to less than a million members. Here again the Anglican church was called to make a unique contribution in the nineteenth century, through the work of the Archbishop of Canterbury's Assyrian Mission, which was sent to Kurdistan at the repeated request of the people themselves, not to draw them from their church and customs, but to give them the means of restoring that old church once more to a state of efficiency.

The present volume is written in an ecumenical spirit, to enlighten the darkness of Western readers about the theology of the Oriental Orthodox churches; their contributions, past and present; the richness of their traditions; their faithfulness to the gospel; the incredible hardships which many of them still experience in their homelands; and the difficulties they have experienced in settling alongside us in the Western world. Contributors to this volume are mostly young Anglican scholars and pastors who, along with others, are dedicating much of their time and energy to the support of these churches in their mission, believing that they have as much, if not more, to share with all of us as we have with them.

How did this book come about? The way was prepared between 1982 and 1984 when, at the request of the Anglican primates, Bishop Henry Hill made three semi-official visits to the heads of the Oriental churches. In June 1982 Bishop Hill, accompanied by John Gibaut as secretary, (now a priest on the Labrador coast) visited Jerusalem and Egypt. Conversations took place with the committee of five bishops who were attempting to guide the Coptic church while Pope Shenouda III was still in detention at the monastery of Bishoy. The discussion centred around the possibility of dialogue and support between our churches. In September of the same year, accompanied this time by Dr Donald M. Schurman (head of the Department of History, RMC, Kingston), Bishop Hill visited His Holiness Vasken I, the Armenian catholicos in Echmiadzin in Soviet Armenia. Later while visiting Colin Battell at St Matthew's Church in Addis Ababa, they met His Holiness Tekle Haimanot, patriarch of Ethiopia in Addis Ababa. The next visit was paid to His Holiness Mar Dinkha IV, catholicos patriarch of the Assyrian Church of the East, at his headquarters in Chicago.

These overtures initially occasioned an element of surprise because the Anglican communion, in distinction to the Church of England, had never before made such visits to the Oriental churches; but each visit was well and hospitably received. The problem then was lack of funds, and when, if at all, Beirut, Damascus, and South India could be visited. However, in July 1983 during the Vancouver assembly of the World Council of Churches, with the able cooperation of Archbishop Paulos Mar Gregorios, metropolitan of Delhi (of the Indian Orthodox church), we were able to arrange an early morning breakfast meeting of representatives of all the churches under the presidency of the archbishop of Canterbury. Anglicans were present from England, Scotland, and Canada. Such was the enthusiasm of the meeting that the Oriental Orthodox and Assyrians, who were also present, accepted an Anglican invitation to attend a theological forum in Great Britain, set for the autumn of 1985.

Meanwhile, in October and November 1984, Bishop Hill made a fourth and final visit to His Holiness Karekin II, at the Armenian catholicosate in Beirut. This was followed by conversations with His Holiness Ignatius Zakka, patriarch of the Syrian Orthodox church in Damascus, and His Holiness Mar Basileus Mar Thoma I Mathews (MT), catholicos of the Indian Orthodox church in Kottayam. William Derby, vicar of Christ Church Cathedral in Montreal, acted as secretary on this occasion.

Such are the bare bones of the visits between our churches. It is quite certain that, had they not taken place, there would have been no forum at St Alban's, England. However, when the forum was held, from 7 to 11 October 1985, all the churches were again represented, and one of the results was the idea of this book. All its chapters, with one exception, are written by forum participants. Anglican representation was selected from different provinces of our communion. Our Eastern brethren, whose names are also recorded, blessed us with such friendship and support that we were encouraged to take this next step. Undoubtedly, the archbishop of Canterbury's address to the participants, in the crypt of Canterbury Cathedral after Evensong on 10 October 1985, sets the correct interpretation of this book.

I am particularly delighted to welcome you all to Canterbury as your meeting is a unique first occasion. Never have Anglicans and representatives of all the Oriental Orthodox churches had such a comprehensive meeting before, although our contacts — and the contacts of the archbishop of Canterbury — go back many years with some of your families.

Anglicans, with good intentions though not always perfect results, offered missions of help to the Syrian churches in the nineteenth century. And there were important visits to this country by Syrian church leaders. Early Lambeth Conferences also urged Anglicans to foster links with the Syrian churches and with the Armenian church. I have myself, as bishop of St Albans, visited both the Armenian catholicoi. More recently we have done what we could to support the largest Christian church in the Middle East, the Coptic Orthodox church, and its pope and patriarch, His Holiness Shenouda III. I have just received a letter from him through His Grace Amba Bishoi, and I deeply appreciate the greetings he has sent me and the support he gives to this forum.

But such contacts as Anglicans have had are still comparatively recent compared with the venerable history of your churches. You go back to the very beginning of Christianity. Your homelands are the homelands of our faith and Christian culture. The founders of your churches were the apostles or their earliest disciples.

Anglicans also greatly admire your constancy in witness during the long years of the Islamic and Ottoman Empires. You are still there at the fountain-place of our faith, but we know that there is no less pressure upon you than in former days. The presence of your diaspora in this country, in Australia, and especially in the New World gives Anglicans much more opportunity to meet your church and learn from you. But we also realize the persecutions and pressures which have driven your peoples out of their homelands to found new communities in a very different culture separated from the wellsprings of your tradition. Among all the Anglican members of the forum, I would also want to specially greet Bishop Samir Kafity because our small church in the Middle East is especially anxious to develop good relations with the ancient mother churches of Christianity. It too knows something of the contemporary religious and political pressures which make Christian witness costly in the Middle East.

Your churches are at the interface of some of the greatest issues facing the world today. Christianity and Islam face each other, and there is an increasing stridency in the followers of the Prophet which makes dialogue more difficult than in former years. In India there is a wider encounter with other faiths as well as the new phenomenon of a Third-World secularism. In Ethiopia the church seeks to play its part in the alleviation of one of the greatest famines in modern times. In that country and also in Armenia the church must find a way of working alongside a theoretically Marxist and atheist state. In Lebanon we see the tragedy of the disintegration of a state in the pressures of competing ideologies and neighbouring powers.

Anglicans salute your courageous witness. I hope this forum will mark the beginning of a more coordinated Anglican sense of solidarity with you as brothers in the faith. And I believe we *are* one in faith.

In spite of our different inheritance in respect to the expression of our doctrine of Christ, I believe we share the same underlying faith. I hope that one day we shall be able to express this together without the language which has divided the West and the Byzantine East from you in the past.

It is important for Christians to show that in spite of different traditions we are one. We need this in the West, with your diaspora, to confront secularism and materialism. You need unity in the East to bear your witness in the face of the politicized and religious pressures put on you. The whole world needs Christians to be united to offer hope for the unity of a humanity divided by class and race, economics and politics, riches and poverty, religion and culture. I welcome you tonight because our Lord prayed for the unity of his disciples so that the world might believe. We must seek unity not only for the sake of the church but for the salvation of the world.

The Armenians

Andrew Mayes and Alan Amos

The ancient Armenian church, with its wide diaspora of an estimated 6 million people, is especially known to other Christians due to the wide persecutions it has been compelled to undergo in the nineteenth and earlier part of the twentieth centuries (during the First World War.) Despite this fragmentation, and despite the political vicissitudes that have deprived it for a time of united leadership, this monastically enriched expression of Christ's church has continued to permeate the daily lives of its children in such a way that church and nationality are often hard to distinguish. Ancient traditions, monks distinguished by their ararat, i.e., pointed cowls, a rich musical heritage, and theological strength make them a recognizably close-knit people whether they appear in Yerevan or Toronto.

Church of England people, and now Anglicans generally, have been and are impressed by the tenacity and liturgical consistency of this resilient people. If it has jurisdictional problems within its ranks, these do not detract from the warmth of the greetings extended to Anglicans from all sections, nor indeed from the courtesies that they extend to each other.

The following chapter details much of the background of the Armenian church and explains its present-day enthusiastic response to ecumenism, especially with Anglicanism. It was written by the Reverend Alan Amos, OBE, MTh, AKC, who was chaplain of All Saints Church, Beirut, Lebanon 1975–82. He is now vice-principal of Westcott House, Cambridge. While in Lebanon he taught English, some church history, and ecumenical studies at the Armenian Orthodox seminary, Bikfaya.

D.S.

The co-author, Reverend Andrew Mayes, BD, a graduate of King's College, London, completed his training for Holy Orders at St Stephen's House, Oxford. He has worked in parishes in London and Essex. At the time of writing he is responsible for the Church of St Thomas of Canterbury, Hullbridge. In 1979-80 he studied at the Armenian seminary of St James in Jerusalem, under the Philip Ussher Memorial scholarship.

H.H.

It is absolutely vital, if one is to understand the Armenian people and their church, to have some grasp of their history. This is so, not for purely academic reasons, but in order to be able to touch the spirit of the Armenians, and to appreciate the essential character of their church.

Armenians are deeply conscious that they are a pilgrim people formed and inspired by a long and hazardous journey. And indeed they are an Easter people, who have tasted often of suffering, to emerge again resurrected: in St Paul's words, ''afflicted but not crushed, struck down but not destroyed: always carrying in the body the death of Jesus, so that the life of Jesus may be manifested in our mortal flesh'' (2 Cor. 8 - 10). If we are to understand the tenacity of the Armenians, their undying dedication to the gospel and the inseparability of church and people, we must know a little of their pilgrimage.[1]

We must begin by asking, where is Armenia? The Armenian homeland, known historically as Greater Armenia, embraced a vast area of mountainous terrain stretching from the Caspian Sea to the east to the Black Sea to the west, from the Caucasus Mountains to the north to the Taurus Mountains to the south. Incredibly fertile and beautiful in parts, it has often been suggested that here is the site of the biblical Garden of Eden, watered by the Tigris. But Armenia is usually known as the land of Ararat, the mountain of Noah's ark dominating the plateau at 1700 feet. The Armenian people themselves are descended from ancient tribes which inhabited this area since prehistoric times. They are an Indo-Aryan people preserving their own ethnic identity and distictive language which holds a special place among Indo-European tongues. Contemporary Armenia consists of a small republic in the Soviet Union, the ancient homeland now lying within Turkish and Iranian borders, its people scattered to the four corners of the world.

Because of its location on one of the most strategic crossroads of the ancient and medieval worlds, Armenia has suffered throughout its history from incursions by many peoples, including the Persians, the Romans, the Arabs, the Turks, and the Russians. Through such vicissitudes the Armenians have been guided and held together by their ancient church which, together with the bonds of language and culture, has been the key to their survival.

Armenians trace the advent of Christianity in their land to the apostolic missions of Bartholomew and Thaddeus, called "the first illuminators of Armenia." This tradition is of vital importance to the Armenians, for it gives to their church both an apostolic foundation and an autocephalous character. Given the location of Armenia and the zeal of those first Christian witnesses, it is certain that the gospel reached its people at an early stage. From the outset Armenian Christians suffered persecutions, beginning with that of the Persian Artaxerxes in AD 110. Deep-rooted paganism and the Sassanid promotion of Mazdaism made for inhospitable conditions for Armenian Christians, but the seeds of faith were surely planted.

It was St Gregory, coming from Caesarea at the end of the third century, who was to be the greatest "Illuminator" of Armenia. After suffering 15 years of imprisonment, he converted King Tiridates who had mercilessly crushed his Christian subjects. Following his baptism, Tiridates proclaimed Christianity the religion of his kingdom, and so in the year 301 Armenia became the first Christian state. As Gregory began his work of evangelization, he had a remarkable vision which has inspired Armenian Christians through sixteen centuries. He saw the opening of heaven, the descent of Christ, and the establishment of a glorious temple with a radiant cross in the centre of the capital city of Vagharshapat. From the edifice flowed abundant streams watering the land of Armenia. Black goats crossed the water becoming white lambs, multiplying in number; wolves attacked, but the lambs were not defeated. Here is encapsulated, in vivid imagery, the whole story of the Armenian church: the vision speaks of the Lord in the midst of his people, of great evangelization, of an autonomous church, of persecution, of triumph. The city of Tiridates was renamed Echmiadzin meaning "the only-

Begotten has descended.'' It is still the centre of the Armenian church and seat of the supreme catholicos, the successor of St Gregory the Illuminator.

After Gregory completed the foundation of the church, the fourth century saw steady building. Because Gregory's successors came to be consecrated not by Caesarean but by Armenian bishops, the church developed its distinctive and independent character. At the synod of Ashtishat in 365, Nerses the Great gave the church a greater organization, promoting its mission among the heathen, and encouraging the growth of monasteries in Armenia. With the invention of the Armenian alphabet in 404 by St Mesrob, the Scriptures, Fathers, and liturgy could be translated for the first time into the language of the people. This proved to be one of the most significant developments in the life of church and nation, for in addition to promoting the growth of a native Armenian literature, it enabled the effective communication of the faith, unifying a widespread people. The production of a standard translation of the Bible in 433 carried this process further.

A common written language and a national church were of vital importance in preserving Armenian unity through times of upheaval. In the fifth century Armenia was divided up between the Byzantines and the Zoroastrian Persians who invaded the country in 451 with a vast army of horsemen and elephants. Thus the Armenian church was hardly free to participate in the Council of Chalcedon meeting that year and so could not consider it fully ecumenical, not all churches being represented. Subsequently, Armenians saw neither the need to add to Cyril of Alexandria's formula at Ephesus in 449 (''one nature united in the Word Incarnate'') nor to become embroiled in political antagonisms.

When from the seventh to the tenth century Armenia was dominated not only by the Byzantines to the west but also by the Muslim Arabs to the east, it was the church that held the people together under the leadership of such outstanding catholicoi as Hovhannes Otzun in the eighth century. Hovhannes, (or John) the Philosopher, as he was called, was both a wise theologian and an able negotiator with the caliph, the Islamic leader. He succeeded in obtaining greater religious freedoms for his people than those allowed in the Covenant of 'Umar which governed Christian activities in this period. Though the Armenian monarchy was revived in the ninth century by the Bagratid dynasty, these remained unsettled times for church and people. The ecclesiastical capital had to be transferred from Echmiadzin to Aghthamar on Lake Van and later to Ani.

In 1064 the Seljuk Turks swept in from Central Asia and Iran opening a new period of instability. Successive catholicoi were again on the move, and Armenians began to emigrate from the homeland in search of peace. Large numbers fled southeastwards to Cilicia, which Armenians began to rule in 1080. The kingdom of Lesser Armenia was established in 1198 and, with its capital at Sis, was approved by both Emperor Henry VI and Pope Celestine II.

During this period Armenians found valued friends in the Crusaders, who too were set against the Muslim Turks, and established closer links with the Church of Rome. Catholicos Nerses Shnorhali the Graceful (1166 – 73) sought to promote ecumenical understanding with the Greeks too. But bitter divisions developed when groups of Catholic "Unitors" and Benedictine missionaries attempted to bring parts of the church into formal union with Rome. The catholicosate at Aghthamar was revived, returning to Echmiadzin in 1441, while the Cilician see of Sis organized itself as a catholicosate ministering to Armenians in the western regions. The wide-flung church was served by two other patriarchates. In Jerusalem, where Armenians had settled since the fifth century, the church developed as a monastic and pilgrim centre, with special responsibilities for the Holy Places. In Constantinople, an Armenian patriarchate was established following the Ottoman invasion of 1451.

Under the domination of the Ottoman Turks, conditions for the church varied immensely. It was organized as a semiautonomous community or Millet which preserved Armenian identity and reinforced the bonds between church and people. But Armenia continued to be a battlefield between the Turks and the Persians, with thousands of its people deported to Isfahan in the seventeenth century. These were often dark days for the church: it could enjoy little dynamic life under these conditions. In the eighteenth century proselytism was renewed by Catholic missionaries leading to the formation of an Armenian Catholic Millet in 1830.

Protestant missionaries were soon to follow. But the nineteenth century also witnessed some impressive advances by the church, such as the establishment of a new seminary at Armash. The National Constitution for the Armenians, agreed upon with the government in 1800, laid down the lines of church organization — giving new responsibilities to the laity — and it survives still in parts of the Middle East.[2]

Meanwhile, church life in eastern Armenia developed within the limits of the Prolojenye regulation formulated by the tsarist government in 1836. Echmiadzin was consolidated as a religious centre, with its monastic institutions, and a new seminary opened during Kevork IV's catholicosate (1866 – 82). But in the reign of his successor Khrimian (1892 – 1907) conditions began to worsen, with the confiscation of some church properties. All this was but a prelude to the darkest chapter in the life of the church in Armenia east and west.

The nineteenth century saw deteriorating conditions for Armenians in Turkey. Vulnerable and unprotected, they sought recognition for basic freedoms, and Western powers began to press the government for urgent reforms; for example at the Berlin Congress in 1878. Conflicts between Armenians and Turks accelerated in the 1890s, and the opening years of the new century saw the massacre of thousands of Armenians. This was only the beginning of a long and unprecedented martyrdom of the Armenians. The Young Turks were soon evolving their pan-Turkish strategy of a purely Turkish empire, while Armenians continued to cherish hopes of autonomy and freedom for church and people. During the First World War the systematic extermination and deportation by the Turks claimed up to one-and-a-half million Armenian lives. Almost one-third of all Armenians perished in what has been called the first genocide of the twentieth century and "the worst calvary that the Armenian people experienced in their history."[3]

After the ensuing tug-of-war between Turkey and Soviet Russia, the frontiers of a small Armenian republic were finally drawn up in 1921. A constitution for Soviet Armenia was settled in 1936. Within restricted freedoms, the church endeavoured to rebuild its life under the leadership of Kevork V "the Sorrowful" and his successors. The patient working out of church-state relationship led to a climate in which, through the dedication of priests and people, the church could be reborn.

Armenian Faith and Religious Life

Belonging to the non-Chalcedonian family of churches, the Armenian church bases its doctrinal understanding of Christ on the conclusions of the first three ecumenical councils of the Christian church, and especially on Cyril of Alexandria's definition ''one nature of the Word Incarnate.'' The Alexandrian school of thought, received principally through the Cappadocian Fathers, was developed within the Armenians' own theological tradition. The Armenian church has produced some outstanding theologians little appreciated in the West because their works in the classical Armenian language remain often untranslated. These include the *Confession of the true and Orthodox faith of the Armenians* by Catholicos Sahag Tsoroporetzi (677 – 703) and the writings of Hovhannes Otzun in the eighth century. The *Book of Questions* by Gregory of Datev in the fourteenth century is considered the *summa theologica* of the Armenian church and gives a precise account of christological beliefs: ''God the Word in His perfection assumed our human nature — soul, body and mind — uniting it with His Deity He became one perfect hypostasis (*antsn*) and one person'' (chapter 7).

Armenian beliefs are richly embodied in the Holy Liturgy which opens with the words, ''O mystery deep, inscrutable, without beginning . . . through the passion of thine holy only-begotten all creation hath been made immortal.''[4] Armenian worship takes place within its distinctive conical-topped churches, with the square altar mounted on a high stage or *bema*. The celebrant, wearing impressive and colourful vestments, is assisted by deacons with censers, acolytes, and singers. The congregation participate in the liturgy fully, sometimes lifting their hands, sometimes bowing low in reverence.

The liturgy itself is the fruit of a long evolution; it derives from the Cappadocian form of the Liturgy of St James of Jerusalem and, besides traces of Byzantine and Latin influence, is a rich compendium of Armenian devotion and theology. It has a dynamic and cosmic character: into the midst comes the Lord Christ who draws the worshipper into the very heart of his sacrifice. It is at once an experience of Calvary and a foretaste of heaven. The drama is heightened by movement and music, with the drawing of a veil across the sanctuary at the most solemn moments and the shaking of fans symbolizing the presence of angels. It is a celebration full of awe, joy, and contemplation; it is other-worldly. The two main moments of the liturgy are the lifting up of the Gospel Book (*"Ase Asdvadz"*: "God is speaking:") to which the people respond in the words of the Nicene Creed, and the procession of the Holy Gifts which is followed by the Hymn of the Kiss of Peace: "Christ in our midst hath been revealed / He who is God is here seated. The voice of peace hath resounded / love is spread over us all." In the liturgy the Armenian people are deeply conscious of their communion with their martyr-saints. Sometimes the music of Gomidas or Ekmalian takes on a plaintive character as past memories are recalled; then it rises joyously as hope and faith in Christ find expression.

Perhaps the most distinctive feature of the Armenian liturgy is the beauty of its hymns and prayers which come in part from the pens of St Nerses the Graceful and St Gregory of Narek. These two writers deserve special attention, for they occupy a prominent place in the popular devotion of the Armenian people and testify to the importance of monasticism as the seed-bed of Armenian spirituality. St Gregory (950 – 1010) lived close to Lake Van at a time when monastic life was flourishing in Armenia. His works, which have lost nothing of their popular appeal for Armenians, spring from the mystical tradition. The *Book of Lamentations* consists of "mystic soliloquies with God," grieving over man's sinful nature and exulting in the unfathomable riches of God's grace: "I who was ruined now stand erect; I was wretched and am victorious, by Christ Jesus and his mighty Father, in the name of the Spirit of truth; unto their unique deity be greatness and glory forever."[5]

St Nerses the Graceful, of the twelfth century, comes too from the monastic tradition and, like Gregory, his prayers spring from a deep appreciation of the Scriptures. His poem "Jesus, Son, Only-Begotten of the Father" is still a widely read spiritual classic inspiring a deep devotion to the Saviour.

A tree in Paradise did grow
But Thou didst bear one on Thy back,
The Cross to set on Golgotha,
The emblem of eternal Hope.
Raise up my fallen, sinful soul
And lay on me Thine easy yoke.[6]

St Nerses, who began important ecumenical exchanges in the twelfth century, can be appreciated now in translation by Christians of all traditions.

Just as Armenians today continue to be inspired by such spiritual writers, so too the church still has monastic life within its bloodstream. What is the state of Armenian monasticism today? One can visit many ruins of monastic churches in Turkey and Soviet Armenia, vestiges of a former glorious tradition. Monastic life was completely disrupted in the last violent decade of the nineteenth century and hundreds of monasteries were destroyed or abandoned during the First World War. Today there is not a single living community surviving in Turkey except for that at Constantinople (Istanbul). There the Monastery of the Holy Cross bravely manages to preserve its life amidst at times oppressive conditions and has a tiny congregation of Armenian nuns, perhaps the only place where an Armenian women's religious order is to be found. There are three other monastic centres in the church — at Holy Echmiadzin; Antelias, Lebanon; and Jerusalem. These all run their own seminaries; so while monastic community life itself is very reduced, priests trained within the monastic tradition are to be found serving in parishes all over the world.

At the heart of every Armenian community is the parish church and centre: the focus not only for rites of passage and spiritual sustenance but of social life as well. The Armenian people, whether in the homeland or in the diaspora, are held together as a family by their participation in the activites of the local church. Special days of celebration, like St Vartan's day (who led the nation in their battle with the Persians in 451) and the memorial of the holocaust on 24 April, further strengthen this deep bond between church and people. The whole year is sanctified by the religious calendar. Christmas, or *Theophany*, is observed on 6

January, preserving the ancient Christian custom of celebrating
the Nativity and Epiphany as one festival of the manifestation
of Christ to the world. The Lenten fast has a special character
in the Armenian church; it is a ''pilgrimage of return,'' a yearn-
ing for paradise lost — while the Palm Sunday liturgies are a pro-
leptic celebration of the Second Coming and the New Age. At
Easter there are special prayers of blessing for Armenians scattered to the four corners of the world.

Since Armenian culture springs from the Christian tradition,
for the Armenian people there is no divide between life and
religion or between nation and church — they are inseparable.
Armenian faith is incarnate in the business of daily living, and
at work or at home Armenians are conscious of their membership in a church which fosters their sense of unity, sustains their
hopes, and maintains their identity wherever they live in the
world.

The Church in Soviet Armenia and Other Historic Centres: A Continuing Ministry

We began our encounter with the Armenians by describing them
as ''a pilgrim people'' who have learnt tenacity and survival
through a tortuous history. What then are the ways in which the
Armenians have striven to make the most of their situation in
the modern world?

First, let us consider Soviet Armenia, the remnant of the
Armenian homeland. Both church and people have had to make
a difficult yet fruitful accommodation to the demands of their
place within the Soviet Union. The circumstances that the
Armenians and their church experienced within the new Soviet
Armenia were not wholly unfamiliar. While Armenians had
benefited in the nineteenth century in some respects from Russian
rule in eastern Armenia (it was certainly preferable for most of
the population to life in western Armenia under the Turks), they
nevertheless had to live with strict limits to their religious
freedom. The tsars had sought to impose Byzantine and Russian
Orthodox practices upon the Armenian church and to discourage
its independence of spirit.

The Soviet government in Armenia was naturally at first rather suspicious of the church and its place in society. While freedom of worship was guaranteed, in other matters, such as education, the role of the church was severly restricted. It is a tribute to the patience, courage, and diplomacy of successive catholicoi that greater liberty has gradually been obtained for the church, particularly since the difficult days of the 1930s. Creative achievements have included the celebration of the fifteen hundredth anniversary of the translation of the Bible into Armenian (in 1935, under the aegis of Catholicos Khoren I), the launching of an official monthly review of the church's activities, *Echmiadzin*, and opening of the theological seminary in Echmiadzin (1944 and 1945, by Catholicos Kevork VI).

The present catholicos, Vazgen I, was elected by the church's conclave in 1955 as the 130th supreme patriarch and catholicos of all Armenians. During his long reign, Catholicos Vazgen has used his gifts of energy and vision effectively in the service of the church in the diaspora as well as in Armenia, making pastoral visits to the Middle East, Europe, the United States, South America, and India, as well as the Armenian dioceses within the Soviet Union such as those in Georgia and Azerbayjan. In 1962, both the catholicosate of Echmiadzin and the catholicosate of Cilicia joined the World Council of Churches, and continue to make a major contribution to the ecumenical movement.

Catholicos Vazgen has actively built up the life of the religious brotherhood in Echmiadzin, developing training at the theological seminary, and has restored churches previously expropriated by the state. Once again the mother church of Armenia — the Cathedral of the Only-Begotten — shines out in splendour, the distinctive conical cupolas crowning a masterpiece of Armenian architecture, while the ancient and beautifully worked *khatchkars* (stone memorial crosses) captivate by their beauty and convey a silent message of victory through suffering. On Sundays, the cathedral resounds to the singing of the Armenian liturgy, which is always well attended. Armenian church music is perhaps easier for Western ears to appreciate than the music of other Eastern churches; with contrasting strands of polyphonic and unison chanting, it portrays in sound the agony and the triumph of Christ and his people.

Through the perseverence of Catholicos Vazgen, the Armenian church has held its ground and found fresh opportunities. In 1961 the patriarchate re-established its printing press, and the *Echmiadzin* monthly and other books on Armenian religion and culture continue to be published, including the Eastern Armenian translation of the New Testament. In recent years, a library and museum has been built to celebrate the rich and varied heritage of Armenian culture.

Armenians remain grateful that within the Soviet Union there is a place for their national life and identity. Furthermore, many Armenians have made a significant contribution to the life of Russia beyond the boundaries of their own republic. Names such as Mikoyan, Khatchaturian, and Kasparov mark achievements by Armenians in spheres as diverse as politics, music, and chess.

Beyond the Armenian homeland, Armenians have had to wrestle with the problems and opportunities of a worldwide dispersion. The earliest important settlement of Armenians outside Armenia itself was in Jerusalem. Just as their own holy city of Echmiadzin bears witness to the reality of the Incarnation, so Armenians through the ages have been drawn to Jerusalem as by a magnet, there to recollect and celebrate the saving events in the life of Christ. Naturally, a settlement of Armenians took root in the city to welcome their pilgrim fellow-countrymen. Testimony is borne to the trek from Armenia to Jersualem by the many pilgrim crosses inscribed in the ancient walls of the Armenian cathedral in Aleppo, Syria, one of the staging-posts of the journey.[7]

The Armenian community in Jerusalem forms a distinct quarter within the walls of the old city. It has witnessed many upheavels through the centuries, and today numbers only about 2,500 people. Nevertheless, the Armenian patriarchate there remains an important centre of learning, worship, and culture in the Holy Land. Under the guidance of the present patriarch, His Beatitude Yegishe Derderian, the theological seminary moved to modern premises in 1971 to continue more effectively its work of receiving new generations of students, many coming from the Armenian community in Turkey, and training them for service in the Middle East and beyond. The patriarchate possesses its own printing press, a museum, and a rare collection of Armenian art treasures which are of international renown. The richly ornate Cathedral of St James makes a striking impression upon visitors to Jerusalem, who may also encounter the monks in their characteristically Armenian robes with pointed hoods leading their choir in services at the Holy Sepulchre, the Church of the Resurrection.

There are many opportunities for ecumenical exchange and encounter in Jerusalem, though due to the conservatism and guardedness of the churches these are only beginning to be explored. The sometimes competitive care of holy places is not always the best introduction to ecumenism. However, of special note is the recent Armenian-Jewish dialogue within the Ecumenical Theological Research Fraternity. Both peoples, having histories of genocide and exile, and having preserved their national identity through bonds of religion and culture, find ground for a common reflection on this experience and an exploration together of their destiny.

Jerusalem has its own particular record of religious and political strife, despite the fervour of pilgrimage and the joy of celebration. Other ancient Armenian settlements also speak of life in adversity, sometimes triumphant, often suffering. We have already referred to the trials which the Armenians experienced at the hands of Byzantines, Arabs, Turks, and Persians, and to the consequent establishment of church centres in Cilicia, Constantinople, and Isfahan. The catholicosate of Cilicia has moved to Lebanon, and its situation and significance will be described when discussing the Armenian diaspora in our century.

The Armenian patriarchate of Constantinople was established ten years after the city fell to the Ottomans. When Sultan Mohammad II occupied Constantinople in 1451, he brought in many Armenians, partly in order to dilute the power of the Greeks but also to encourage commerce and crafts. The patriarchate of Constantinople has naturally been profoundly affected by the massacres and deportations from Western Armenia earlier this century, and its role is necessarily much less than it was in former times. However, Patriarch Schnorhk (elected 1961) has the delicate task of maintaining the continuing Armenian religious presence in Istanbul (Constantinople) and relating to the Turkish authorities on behalf of his community. Along with Jerusalem,

Constantinople depends spiritually on the catholicosate of Echmiadzin.

An Armenian presence in Isfahan, Iran, dates from the invasion of Armenia by the Persian king Shah Abbas in 1605. He deported large numbers of Armenians to his capital, where they settled and prospered, building their own city of New Julfa and introducing the art of printing into Persia. The churches of New Julfa are of outstanding beauty and interest. The Armenian archbishopric of Isfahan, dependent on the catholicosate of Cilicia, has continued its ministry under the Iranian revolution and the new circumstances which have arisen. Armenians are respected in Iran because of their long-standing presence in the country and their ancient civilization. Protestant churches, with their more recent origin and links with Western missions, have suffered greater hostility.

The Twentieth-Century Diaspora

Up to the twentieth century, the two most active centres of the Armenian church were the catholicosate of Echmiadzin and the patriarchate of Constantinople, recognized by the Ottoman authorities as the centre of the Armenian church in the empire. As for the catholicosate of Cilicia, it played a much more limited role, having its seat in Sis (the capital of the ancient kingdom of Cilicia) and exercising jurisdiction over Cilicia, Syria, and Cyprus.

With the First World War the suffering of the Armenians in their native lands reached a climax, and they were forced by the Turks to flee eastward into Russia or southward to the shelter of the British and French armies. In 1921 Cilicia itself was evacuated; Robert Brenton Betts writes:

> By 1925 some 150,000 Armenians were found huddled and destitute on the outskirts of Beirut, crowded into their ancient but tiny quarters in Aleppo, Damascus, and Baghdad, and resolutely building makeshift shelters in what were then the open wastes of the Jazira (North Syria). Aided by the French Mandate government, by Armenian, European, and American

charities, and in the final analysis by their unbroken will to survive, these homeless refugees were within one generation securely established in the Levant as a growing and thriving community, and an economic force to be reckoned with wherever they had sunk roots.[8]

In 1930 the catholicosate of Cilicia established itself at Antelias on the outskirts of Beirut. Even as the scope of the patriarchate in Constantinople had been reduced with the collapse of the Ottoman Empire and the massacre and expulsion of so many Armenians, so the new situation of the catholicosate of Cilicia led to fresh responsiblities and challenges.

Sahak I, catholicos of Cilicia at the time of the move to Lebanon, had been deeply affected by the terrible sufferings of his people. In 1931, therefore, he called upon a younger man, Archbishop Babgen Guleserian, to assist him as coadjutor catholicos. During the next five years a seminary was established at Antelias and a printing press set up to publish a monthly review as well as other religious, educational, and historical publications.

Later, the cathedral of Antelias, the memorial chapel of the Armenian martyrs, the residence of the catholicos, and the seminary building were erected. The Second World War halted this period of construction, but from 1945 onwards there was a cultural renewal in the life of the catholicosate, including the training of increased numbers of theological students. The reign of Catholicos Zareh I (1956 – 63) marked a fresh departure: the ministry of the catholicosate was extended to further Armenian communities in the diaspora, to Iran, Greece, and a part of the community in the United States. Admittedly, this was beyond the bounds of the sphere of influence traditionally accorded to the catholicosate of Cilicia, and this new activity led to a deterioration of relations between Cilicia and Echmiadzin, which was historically responsible for ministry to the wider diaspora, being the mother see of the Armenian church. The international political climate contributed to these difficulties; many Armenians in countries whose governments were hostile to the Soviet Union were reluctant to relate directly to the church in Soviet Armenia and, of course, Armenian emigrants from Lebanon and Syria already had a relationship with the catholicosate of Cilicia. With the easing of political tensions and expressions of good will on both sides, a more positive relationship has developed between Echmiadzin and Cilicia, though the dispute has not been finally resolved.

At first the reign of Catholicos Khoren I Panoyen (1963 – 83) marked the consolidation of the Armenian presence in Lebanon and the strengthening of the life of the catholicosate. However, from 1975 onwards the Armenian community in Lebanon has been through times of trial and suffering, being caught in the cross-fire of the Lebanese conflict. A priority has been to support the legitimate Lebanese authorities and to avoid inter-Armenian clashes between rightist and leftist factions.[9] The Armenian church developed a policy of ''positive neutrality'' within the Lebanese situation and thus sought to make a real contribution towards steering Lebanon away from self-destruction. However, the Armenian reluctance to be wholly identified with either side in the sectarian violence has placed them in an increasingly vulnerable position. They have in the past incurred the anger of extremist Christian organizations, while recent reports (summer 1986) speak of assaults and murders of several Armenian shopkeepers in West Beirut, obviously with the aim of driving the community out of an area where they have lived peaceably among Muslims for several decades.

Words are incapable of expressing the sadness of the Armenian plight in Lebanon; a people which has borne such persecution earlier in this century has now found itself again a target for men of violence and fanaticism. Both in Cyprus and in Lebanon — places where the Armenians had seemed able to establish peaceful and prosperous communities — devastation has been the fate of many. Not surprisingly, such experiences and the sense of deep insecurity which they generate have hastened the stream of Armenian emigration from the Middle East: emigration from lands where Armenian culture has had the chance of establishing itself, to lands where there is always the danger of becoming ''not a people.'' It is particularly tragic that the currents of history should be driving so many Armenians from the Middle East at a time when the church has such a strong and imaginative leader there in the person of Catholicos Karekin II. Elected in 1977 as catholicos-coadjutor to Khoren I, and assuming full leadership of the catholicosate of Cilicia since Khoren's death in 1983, Karekin II has played a notable role in the ecumenical movement, both internationally, as one of the vice-moderators of the World Council of Churches (1975 – 1983), and regionally, as a focal figure in the Middle East Council of Churches' quest for reconciliation in Lebanon. A man of personal humility and warmth, Karekin II has always determined that his high office should not oust his desire to be both pastor and friend to all those he encounters, whether they are members of the Armenian community or not.

The Wider Diaspora

The numerical strength of the Armenian communities throughout the world can only be estimated very roughly. "Seven million people say *Ayo!*" (the Armenian for "Yes") proclaimed a report published in Vienna in 1975. It was perhaps a flourish of optimism, and yet other calculations are by now moving in that direction. One authority gives a figure of approximately 3,000,000 Armenians living in Soviet Armenia, about 1,500,000 in the other republics of the Soviet Union, and perhaps 2,000,000 in the diaspora.[10] This would mean a world total of 6,500,000 Armenians, and such is the initiative and adventurous spirit of the Armenians that there must be very few countries that have not encountered them. The constraints of space mean that this discussion of Armenian communities in the wider diaspora is inevitably very brief.[11]

The lure of freedom, prosperity, and equality provided by the U.S.A. has been a major attraction to Armenian emigrants. Today the highest concentration of Armenians in the United States is around Los Angeles. Armenians have been notable in the business world, in literature (for example Saroyan and Michael Arlen), in athletics, science, and musical circles. There are a substantial number of books and newspapers published in Armenian, both by the church and by the Armenian political parties. Church life has been much encouraged by the establishment of the seminary of St Nerses (1962) now linked with St Vladimir's Orthodox Seminary in New York.

There are also notable Armenian communities in the main cities of Canada, while in South America substantial Armenian communities can be found in Uruguay, Venezuela, Brazil, and the Argentine.

Perhaps the Armenian community with the longest history in Europe is that of France. Armenian links with France go back to the Crusades, and Leon V, the last king of Lesser Armenia, is buried at St Denis. In Great Britain the Manchester Armenian community has roots going back to the 1840s and the expansion of the textile industry. There are Armenians who are equally at home in Manchester and in Aleppo, Syria, and who switch from Mancunian English to Syrian colloquial Arabic to modern Armenian with chameleon-like ease. They wear their internationalism lightly and with a touch of humour. The Armenian community in London has increased in recent years, due to the Turkish invasion of Cyprus and the troubles in Lebanon. In London there are now two Armenian churches and an Armenian cultural centre. The Armenian bishop in London represents the supreme catholicos to the archbishop of Canterbury. London benefits frequently from the talents of Armenian musicians such as the violinist Manoug Parikian.

Of other West European settlements of Armenians, those in Italy, West Germany, Austria, and Switzerland are of particular note. The settlement in Italy reflects the historical importance of relations between the papacy and the Armenian people. The Armenian Catholic order of the Mekhitarists (founded by Mekhitar of Sebaste over 250 years ago in Istanbul) maintains a monastery on the island of Saint Lazaro, Venice. The reputation of the order for its work in scholarship and education has won the respect of all Armenians.

Since the Middle Ages Armenians have been involved in trade, diplomacy, and mission with India, the Far East, and Africa. There was a particularly thriving Armenian community in Bombay and Calcutta during the days of the British Empire. Most interestingly, there is a long-established Armenian connection with Ethiopia. Due to the theological and ecclesiastical links between the Armenian church and the national church of Ethiopia, Bishop Derenik Poladian (murdered 1963) was for some years dean of the Ethiopian seminary in Addis Ababa.

To Survive Creatively: The Contemporary Challenge

Armenians today continue their age-long struggle to make the best of their circumstances, whatever those may be. This is true, whether it means accepting the limited freedoms of life in Soviet Armenia, the hazards of continuing as a Christian minority in the Middle East — facing the strong reactionary currents in contemporary Islam — or prospering in the Western diaspora with the ever-present risk of loss of communal or personal sense of identity.

The Armenian people also bear within them their grievance against Turkey for its refusal to accept any responsiblity for the genocide, as well as a disillusionment at the indifference of other nations to their own deprivation of nationhood. It is not surprising that in a world which is beset by violent political movements, this resentment has led to acts of violence against Turkish interests in the West, largely undertaken by members of the younger generation, often under the auspices of the Armenian Secret Army for the Liberation of Armenia (ASALA). The reaction of Western countries has been simply to class such Armenians with the generality of violent Middle Eastern movements, rather than look deeper into the causes of such violence. It is a shame that so often in the Western media prominence is given to Armenian activity only if it is the stuff of news headlines. It has given the average Westerner a totally distorted impression of Armenian life and values. Often the Armenian church is called upon to condemn terrorist acts. It does indeed refuse to condone this recourse to lawless violence, but also feels obliged to point to the much greater violence within twentieth-century history which has produced such a reaction. There is a gulf of incomprehension between the Western liberal and the young Armenian activist, who feels obliged to hope for eventual justice for his nation — some day, some time — and may be tempted into unreasonable action to avoid the abyss of doing nothing.

For the Armenian church itself there is clearly the need to arouse the conscience of the world concerning the injustice to Armenians. There is also the need to reflect theologically on the role of the Armenian nation through history and the significance of the martyrdom of its people in the twentieth century. Westerners are often strangely insensitive to these needs, and yet, if they had suffered the experience of having a third of their civilian population wiped out within living memory, they would be facing precisely the same challenge.

While for the Armenians the disaster of the massacres has not been followed by the final trauma of assimilation and extinction, such a fate can only be avoided in the diaspora by a consciousness of their call to witness to their own true identity in their daily living. The New Testament word for witness is *martyria*, and it is only in the deepest understanding of this equation that a relevant theology can be born: "the history of the Armenian Church is the most eloquent testimony of what can be called witness through living martyrdom and a spirit of creativeness."[12]

At times in this history, the struggle to survive has had to be the great priority; today, in the diaspora, the struggle continues in a different form. In Western countries, many of the younger generation are no longer fluent in the Armenian language and are attracted to conformity with the lifestyle and ethos of the host country. The Armenian church, as it struggles to survive to future generations in such an environment, finds its own renewal in refusing both the retreat into a "ghetto" style of existence and the radical alienation which the unquestioning acceptance of social trends would bring. It may be that its vocation is to bear witness as a faithful remnant at the heart of a more dispersed and less definable Armenian presence — a witness to the grace of God prevailing through the tribulations of a nation's history and his presence with them on their pilgrimage.

Anglican-Armenian Relations

Both the Anglican communion and the Armenian church are committed to the ecumenical vision and to developing closer relationships based on mutual trust and greater understanding of each other's traditions. Successive Lambeth Conferences have resolved to pursue every avenue which can lead to greater unity, while the Armenian church, through its episcopal conferences at Echmiadzin and in other ways, has reiterated its preparedness to strengthen existing bonds of friendship. This friendship has manifested itself in all sorts of ways, including exchange visits between heads of churches, participation in the wider forum of the WCC, and in collaboration at the parish level. Several paths are already being pursued, but there remain many which are still unexplored. We will consider these under three main heads: the experiences of shared worship, academic and educational exchanges, and pastoral cooperation.

The life of prayer
First and foremost is the need to appreciate each other's forms of worship and spirituality. This is vital for many reasons. Theology is rightly expressed and celebrated in living liturgy: in sharing in prayer and worship one is drawn into the very heart of a church's life and can begin to understand its history and its hopes at the deepest level. Further, participation together in worship affirms the spiritual communion that already exists between churches by virtue of our common baptism and strengthens the experience of fellowship in Christ. Many Anglicans have been able to appreciate the beauty and depth of the Armenian liturgy, which embodies the spirituality of the centuries, and some have been able to witness such special ceremonies as the seven-yearly Blessing of the Oils at Holy Echmiadzin. Others of us may recollect the foot-washing in the Liturgy of Holy Thursday (an experience which Anglicans have come to explore in their own revised liturgies), or the magnificent celebration of the Armenian Christmas-Epiphany, culminating in the pouring of holy oil from the beak of a silver dove into the baptismal waters. In Beirut, the perils of crossing the green line under sniper fire to attend the celebration were assuaged by entry into heaven once one reached Antelias! Jerusalem as a place of pilgrimage also affords the opportunity to witness Armenian celebrations in the Holy Places.

At parish level there have also been many occasions when Anglican and Armenian congregations have shared in acts of worship, both in the Week of Prayer for Christian Unity and at other times, such as the Armenian National Martyrs' Day. Easily available English translations of the Armenian liturgy, together with transliterations of the Armenian text, have enabled a greater degree of participation in the eucharistic celebration. Anglicans now realize that they are welcome in Armenian churches as visitors and will be greeted cordially by the local priest and congregation. Likewise Armenians have encountered not only the riches of the *Book of Common Prayer* but also the renewed liturgies as they have developed in different parts of the Anglican communion. They have often attended occasions such as the consecration of a bishop and special parish celebrations. They are assured of a loving reception and will be offered the sign of peace as fellow-members of the body of Christ even though full intercommunion has not yet been achieved.

In very special circumstances limited "eucharistic hospitality" has been permitted. As E.F.K. Fortescue relates, "the late Catholicos Nierces, when in Bagdad in 1814, finding that no English clergymen were present in the country, attended several Englishmen on their deathbeds and administered Holy Communion to them requiring them only to confess their belief in the Trinity and in the Real Presence in the Holy Eucharist."[13] When Armenian refugees settling in the U.S.A. at the end of the last century found themselves without local Armenian priests, they were welcomed to Holy Communion in parts of the Episcopal church.

The question of eucharistic hospitality was briefly raised by Archbishop Coggan during his visit to Catholicos Vazgen I at Echmiadzin in 1977. It is hoped that guidelines can be agreed upon between the churches for circumstances where Anglicans or Armenians find themselves geographically separated from their own churches.

A little-explored way in which the inner life of the churches can be appreciated is through the prayerful reading of spiritual writers: some important works are already available in translation. Through attending to each other's spiritual fathers, we can begin to fathom the depths of our traditions of prayer and to appreciate the inseparability of prayer and theology. The monastic traditions of the two churches have much to explore in this regard, leading perhaps to regular exchanges between monasteries and convents. Retreats could be undertaken for religious orders and secular congregations by a member of the other church.

Academic study

The second major area of ecumenical cooperation is that of academic study. Mutual understanding is based on the foundation of learning , and in the past relations have been held back by a lack of knowledge of each other's traditions. Since the Second World War, however, many opportunities for serious study have been recognized and seized.

Today there are four main seminaries in the Armenian church, each springing from the monastic tradition: St Gregory, Echmiadzin; the Seminary of the Catholicosate of Cilicia, Bikfaya, Lebanon; St James, Jerusalem; and Holy Cross school, Istanbul (which is sadly depleted due to local conditions); in addition, there is the theological school of St Nerses Shnorhali at St Vladimir's seminary in New York. Anglicans, lay and ordained, have participated in Armenian theological education both as students and as teachers of English and ecumenics, and have been enabled not only to undertake serious study but also to share in Armenian community life and in its monastic resources. Similarly, Armenian students for the priesthood have completed their studies in Anglican institutions, and a number have undertaken postgraduate research, so that many of the present generation of Armenian clergy have had close contacts with the Anglican heritage.

All this is but a beginning, and there are several ways in which mutual learning can be promoted. Firstly, theological publications and church newspapers could be systematically exchanged between colleges. There is an urgent need for Armenian literature in English, and many look forward to the publication in translation of the official organ *Echmiadzin* and to more material from the Armenian publishing houses in the U.S.A. Secondly, there could be a greater exchange of lecturers between colleges, either for a term or a series of addresses or sabbaticals. Thirdly, charitable educational bodies could explore further the possiblity of providing scholarships and sponsorships, to enable a two-way exchange of graduate students. Fourthly, Anglican theological curricula could include a definite place for the history, liturgy, and spirituality of the Armenian and other Oriental churches, to acquaint students in the course of their general studies as well as to encourage specialist study.[14] Armenian seminaries could similarly consider teaching about the Anglican church and its theological tradition in the context of the ecumenical movement.

On another level, it is hoped that further theological conversations between the two churches can be arranged, leading to the establishment of a formal dialogue or doctrinal commission. This has been a long-cherished hope of successive Lambeth Conferences and of the Armenian episcopate alike. The 1948 conference asked the archbishop of Canterbury to ''seek to initiate discussions between theologians of the two Churches, to be appointed by himself and by the Supreme Catholicos of the Armenians, with the view to strengthening the relations between the two Churches.''[15] Plans were formulated for theological conversations on christological issues to take place in Jerusalem in 1958, but were never realized due to local difficulties.

Both churches are engaged in dialogue through the World Council of Churches,[16] but it is hoped that a small group of scholars from both churches could meet to lay the foundations either for bilateral conversations or for dialogue between the whole family of Oriental Orthodox churches and the Anglican communion. The theological traditions of the two churches have evolved in different ways, and dialogue would seek to uncover the fundamental unity of faith that already exists. In particular, the Armenian church and the Church of England have both developed as national churches, and there is much to share within the debate on faith and culture.

Such possibilities for dialogue were raised briefly by Archbishop Coggan in his meetings with Catholicos Vazgen in 1975 and 1977, and by Archbishop Runcie in his more recent contacts. There is much work to be done, including finding the financial resources to support such a project, but both churches are encouraged by their mutual readiness to enter into formal dialogue at the opportune time.

Pastoral support
A third major way in which interchurch relations have been strengthened has been in the area of mutual pastoral support. Again this has manifested itself on all sorts of levels. As St Paul wrote, ''When one member of the body of Christ suffers, all

members suffer together.'' During the period of Armenian persecutions, the Anglican church identified with their brethren through various expressions of sympathy and encouragement, and by pastoral support where it was possible.

This began with earnest intercession for the Armenian church, such as that shared with Patriarch Zaven of Istanbul in London in 1920. At the height of the massacres, the archbishop of Canterbury, Randall Davidson, made several representations on behalf of the Armenians, and was conferred with the First Order of St Gregory the Illuminator by Catholicos Kevork V in recognition of his endeavours. At this time various church members in London were engaged in fund raising to aid refugees fleeing from Turkey. In more recent times, Anglican representatives have made a contribution within the World Council of Churches, which is recognizing an ecumenical responsibility in relation to the unresolved issues of the genocide.

With the growth of the Armenian diaspora and the establishment of Armenian emigrant communities all over the world have come many more opportunities for pastoral cooperation. There is much to share within several vital areas of mutual interest, especially on this local, informal level. More attention should be given within local councils of churches and ecumenical fraternals to such issues as the training of youth in Christian discipleship, evangelism, the nurture of the Christian family, and the care of the bereaved. Where Anglican and Armenian churches find themselves close neighbours within cities, there may be scope for joint welfare projects and the pooling of resources and ideas. Certainly there are many avenues of collaboration still to be investigated; partnerships in ministry in the community can be considered as local clergy and lay leaders meet more frequently together and develop trust and friendship. Joint meetings between respective parish councils might be arranged at regular intervals, to promote a greater exchange of ideas and the chance to explore concrete acts of common witness and pastoral care.

The sharing of churches and altars has been one such expression of practical support in the local community and a symbol of greater openness between the churches. In London, North America, and elsewere, Anglican churches have been made available to Armenians on a permanent basis, facilitating worship and the development of community life. In the East, Anglicans have been allowed to celebrate the eucharist in their own rite at Armenian altars, for example in Istanbul. Many pastoral links have developed between the churches through chaplaincies serving Anglicans living abroad, especially in the Middle East.

Armenian faith, prayer, and history have become incarnate in a rich and distinctive culture often too little appreciated in the West. The eventful pilgrimage of the Armenian people through the centuries has been marked by a creative activity in the arts, manifest in magnificent architecture, classical literature, finely illustrated manuscripts, and resplendent liturgy. All this springs from the experience and gifts of a church which has held together its people through many vicissitudes; in Armenian culture one can discern the shades of sorrow and the light of faith. Different ways of presenting these riches should be explored; increased opportunities for contact with such tangible expressions of the Armenian experience can help Anglicans and others to understand more deeply the spirit of the people or introduce them to the church for the first time.

Perhaps the idea of local festivals of Armenian culture could be investigated — celebrations of the unique Armenian contribution to civilization. Anglican cathedrals, in cities where there is an established Armenian presence, could host well-publicized events such as exhibitions and concerts, or perhaps a celebration of the Armenian liturgy. This would enable a higher profile for the Armenian people that could not only make an invaluable contribution to ecumenism but also give access to the Armenian heritage for large numbers of people.

The Armenian diaspora has brought many new opportunities for contact with the West: we are no longer distant friends but close neighbours. Today, as never before in the history of our two churches, we have the chance to learn together of our different traditions, for now, in so many places in the world, Anglican and Armenian Christians live side by side. We are called to tread together the path of Christian discipleship in faith and love. We are called, too, to build upon the solid foundations of trust and friendship that have been laid.

Endnotes

1 The following paragraphs are indebted to the fine account in Aziz Atiya, *A History of Eastern Christianity*. In this first section we trace the history of the church to the foundation of the Soviet Republic of Armenia in 1921. For recent history and contemporary life, see section III of this essay.

2 For recent history see K. Sarkissian, "The Armenian Church in Contemporary Times," *Religion in the Middle East*, ed. A. J. Arberry (Cambridge University Press, 1969).

3 Arberry, p. 490.

4 The Hymn of Vesting in *The Divine Liturgy* Armenian Church of America, 3rd ed. (New York, 1974).

5 Elegy II *Lamentations of Narek*, trans. M. Kudian (London: Mashtots Press, 1977), p. 47.

6 Nerses Shnor'hali St, *Jesus, Son and only Begotten of the Father*, reordered into English by Jane S. Wingate (New York: Delphic Press, 1947).

7 By the 7th century the Armenians had built as many as 70 monasteries in the Holy Land, according to the contemporary monk Haroutoun. See K. Hintlian, *History of the Armenians in the Holy Land* (Jerusalem: St. James' Press, 1976), p. 16.

8 Robert Brenton Betts, *Christians in the Arab East* (Athens: Lycabettus Press, 1978), p. 55.

9 There are strong cross-currents of political opinion among Armenians, and rival political parties owe their origins to Ottoman days: e.g., the Dashnak (pro-Western nationalists), the Ramgavar (liberals), and the Hentchak (socialists in sympathy with Soviet Armenia). These labels fail to do justice to the complexities of Armenian politics; for some guidance see Christopher Walker's comments in *Armenia, The Survival of a Nation* (London: Croom Helm, 1980).

10 Bishop Berberian, "The Armenian Apostolic Church," *Martyria Mission: the witness of the Orthodox churches today*, ed. Ion Bria (Geneva: WCC, 1980), pp. 207 ff.

11 For further detail see "The Armenians," Minority Rights Group, Report no. 32, (revised 1981 edition), pp. 16 ff.; also *Histoire des Armeniens* ed. Gerard Dedeyan (Toulouse: Editions Privat, 1982), esp. ch. 16.

12 Very Revd. Aram Keshishian, "The Armenian Church in Diaspora," *Martyria/Mission*, p. 213.

13 E.F.K. Fortescue, *The Armenian Church* (London: 1872; rpt. New York: AMS Press, 1970) p. 220.

14 See "Statement of the Conference of the Heads of the Oriental Orthodox Churches Addis Ababa 1965" in K. Sarkissian, *The Witness of the Oriental Orthodox Churches* (Beirut, 1968).

15 Resolution 686.

16 See *Background Information Commission of the Churches on International Affairs* (WCC, 1984), p. 32.

The Copts

Geoffrey Rowell

The Coptic Orthodox Church was born in apostolic times; its teachers and martyrs were foremost among leaders of the early church. Indeed the Coptic calendar has its beginnings in the great persecution of Diocletian at the end of the third century. Overwhelmed by successive Moslem Arab invasions in the eighth and ninth centuries, it was largely forgotten by its sister churches in the west until nineteenth-century missionaries, to their great surprise, rediscovered its teaching and witness. In our own time we are rediscovering the spirituality of the desert fathers and mothers.

His Holiness Pope Shenouda III, the present patriarch of Alexandria and the 118th successor of St Mark, exemplifies so much of the story which Canon Geoffrey Rowell relates in this chapter.

The meeting of Dr Robert Runcie, the current archbishop of Canterbury, with Pope Shenouda III and their signing of a common declaration 10 July 1987 highlighted the relationship of this ancient church with the churches of the Anglican communion. They began with a common declaration of the Nicene faith; they touched on past misunderstandings of the Incarnation of our Lord, "who is Perfect in His Divinity and Perfect in His Humanity in a real and perfect union without mingling or commixture, without confusion or change, without division or separation, His Divinity did not separate from His Humanity for an instant. He who is God eternal and invisible became visible in the flesh, and took upon Himself the form of a servant."

They then expressed the need to examine within the Anglican/Oriental Orthodox pastoral forum established in 1985, difficulties and misunderstandings regarding the sacrament of Holy Baptism. A future theological forum should provide a place for discussion of this and other difficulties preventing closer relations and ultimate communion between our two churches.

The Reverend Dr Geoffrey Rowell is fellow, chaplain, and tutor in theology at Keble College, Oxford, and a university lecturer in theology. He is a canon of Chichester Cathedral and a member of the Church of England Liturgical Commission. He has for many years had a personal interest in the Oriental Orthodox churches and in 1979 spent two months in the Monastery of St Macarius in the Wadi el-Natroun.

H.H.

The ancient Christian church of Egypt, known to Western Christians as the Coptic church (*Copt* being derived from the Greek *aiguptos*, an Egyptian), traces its foundation to the preaching of St Mark the Evangelist in Alexandria, where Coptic tradition states he was martyred in AD 68. Alexandria had long been the home of a large Jewish community, and from Alexandrian Judaism came the Greek translation of the Old Testament we know as the Septuagint. Also from Alexandria came Philo, a contemporary of Jesus, whose writings mark the engagement of Judaism with Platonic philosophy. From the reference in St. Matthew's Gospel to Mary and Joseph fleeing with the infant Jesus into Egypt comes another important theme in Coptic tradition. At Matarieh in Cairo the Virgin's tree is still pointed out as marking the place where the Holy Family stayed, and similar holy places associated in Coptic tradition with the sojourn of the Holy Family in Egypt are found at various points along the Nile. Ethiopian tradition elaborated this journey to bring the Holy Family to Ethiopia.

The martyrdom of St Mark, the reverence accorded to the Virgin Mary, and the learning of Alexandria are all marks of the Coptic church. In the early centuries it was Alexandria which became one of the great centres of Christian thought, particularly through the great catechetical school established there at least by the year AD 190. Clement, and above all Origen, shaped Christian thought and devotion, Origen contributing both as a student of the Bible and a systematic theologian striving to express Christian truth in the philosophical terminology of the Hellenistic world. After

Origen, at the beginning of the fourth century, Athanasius became the leading opponent of Arianism (which also had its origins in Alexandria) and fought tenaciously for the full divinity of Christ, the Son of God who had become man that we might be made "partakers of the divine nature." A century later it was to be another bishop of Alexandria, Cyril, who insisted on the full and complete unity of the person of Christ, "the Word made flesh," teaching that the union of the divinity and humanity was at the most fundamental level of Christ's being, and favouring the theological formula "the one nature of the incarnate Word." The creeds of Christendom bear the stamp of the great thinkers of Alexandria, and so of the Egyptian church.

Learning and theological disruption were characteristic of the church of Alexandria in the early centuries; but the theme of martyrdom was also present. The church historian, Eusebius of Caesarea, records that the persecution of Decius fell with particular severity on Egypt, and there are many accounts of martyrdoms from the great persecution of Diocletian and Maximian at the beginning of the fourth century. The accounts of the martyrs often took a standardized common form; features include the martyrdom being sought voluntarily as the result of a specific divine command, a sequence of tortures, a Nile journey, and (in the case of St George, sometimes several resurrections) until the martyr finally succumbs being "fatigued with dying." With the cessation of persecution and the accession of Constantine, the veneration of the martyrs assumed a prominent place in popular Coptic practice. The relics of the martyrs were accorded high honour, and each local church sought to have the shrine and place of pilgrimage for at least one such saint. In the fifth century the monastic reformer Shenoute was critical of certain aspects of this martyr cult, alleging that the need for each village to have its martyr's shrine had meant that "the bones of some nameless dead were disinterred and assumed to be the relics of martyrs and honoured accordingly, without any reliable evidence that they were ever the remains of Christians."[1]

With the establishment of Christianity as the official religion of the Roman Empire, the early period of persecution ceased. The faith which has sustained Christians in the face of torture and death now found a new expression for some in a response to

God's inner call to the ascetic life of the desert. Abandoning the settled life of the Nile Valley, the first Christian monks withdrew to caves on the desert escarpment or to remoter parts of the desert to wrestle with the demonic powers thought to inhabit the wilderness, and to devote themselves completely to Christ, renouncing the power and possessions that the world offered. St Anthony, revered as "the father of monks," hearing the gospel, "If thou wilt be perfect sell what thou hast and give to the poor and come, follow me," withdrew to the desert about the year 269 when he was a young man of twenty. At his death in 356 he had drawn many to follow a similar life and was venerated for his spiritual wisdom. To the brethen at Arsinoe Anthony wrote:

> My dear children, I pray . . . that you may not grow weary of loving one another. Lift up your body in which you are clothed, and make it an altar, and set thereon all your thoughts, and leave there every evil counsel before the Lord, and lift up the hands of your heart to Him . . . and pray to God that He may grant you His great invisible fire, that it may descend from heaven, and consume the altar and all that is on it, and that all the priests of Baal, who are the contrary works of the enemy, may fear and flee from your face as from the face of Elijah the prophet. And then you will see a cloud "like a man's hand" over the sea, which will bring you the spiritual rain, which is the comfort of the Comforter Spirit.[2]

The ascetic life of the desert is a thirsting for the living water of the Spirit and a sacrificial offering in love to God. Anthony in his cave is seen as the prototype of the solitary, hermit life.

Pachomius, a comtemporary of Anthony's, is revered as the father of monastic community life, from the example of his Christian community at Tabbenesi in Upper Egypt. Of that community life one who looked back on it wrote, "We were not conscious of living on earth but of feasting in heaven." What was that community life like? The monks woke early, summoned by a horn or gong, having slept in their cells propped up on special seats, designed to prevent undue length of sleep. Gathering together, the community would begin the morning prayer, consisting of extensive readings of scripture followed by the Lord's Prayer and periods of silent reflection. As they worked during the day, the monks would recite texts of Scripture, drawing down the text into the heart. All were expected to learn at least some of the Psalter and the New Testament. Work was divided so that no one became attached to a particular job. Basket-weaving and the making of ropes and mats were characteristic activities, as well as work in the fields attached to the monastery. The main meal was taken in the middle of the day, and a lighter one in the evening. After the evening meal Pachomius would deliver his instruction, and then, before retiring to their cells, the monks would return to their "houses" (a group of twenty cells) for further prayer and discussion of the instruction they had been given. On Sundays and feast days when the Eucharist was celebrated, there was a special emphasis on the psalms and singing. Of this life Horseios, one of Pachomius's disciples wrote:

> Our father (Pachomius) strengthened us from the Scriptures through his perfect knowledge. But I think, in my poverty that if a man does not guard his heart well, he forgets and neglects all that he has had. And so the enemy finds a place in him and casts him down.[3]

The desert fathers, as we shall see, have remained a powerful influence in the tradition of the Coptic church, as well as bequeathing a rich inheritance of prayer and spirituality to the whole of Christendom. Their pithy and epigrammatic responses to those who journeyed into the desert to seek their advice have a directness and often an ingenuousness which is both challenging and attractive. The church historian, Sozomen, gives us a picture of the monks of Nitria and the Cells, the area to the west of the Nile Delta.

> Nitria, inhabited by a great number of persons devoted to a life of philosophy . . . contains about fifty monasteries, built tolerably near to each other, some of which are inhabited by monks who live together in a society, and others by monks who have adopted a solitary mode of existence. More in the interior of the desert, about seventy stadia from this locality,

is a region called the Cells, throughout which numerous little dwellings are dispersed hither and thither, but at such a distance that those who dwell in them can neither see nor hear each other. They assemble together on the first and last days of each week; and if any monk happens to be absent it is immediately concluded that he is ill, or has been attacked by some disease, and all the monks visit him alternately, and carry such remedies as are suited to his case. Except on these occasions, they seldom converse together, unless, indeed, there be one among them capable of communicating further knowledge concerning God and the salvation of the soul. Those who dwell in the cells are those who have attained to the summit of philosophy (i.e., spiritual wisdom), and who are therefore able to regulate their own conduct, to live alone, and to seek nothing but quietude.[4]

Cyril, patriarch of Alexandria from 412 to 444, stressed, as we have seen, the unity of the person of Christ and the fact that, whatever else might be said about Jesus, it was the divine Word who was the subject of the person of Christ. He suspected his rival, Nestorius, of teaching a doctrine of "two sons"   a Christ not fully and completely united, what one might colloquially refer to as a "schizoid Christ." Nestorius was condemned at the Council of Ephesus in 431. Cyril's teaching was affirmed, but the later Council of Chalcedon, held in 451 after Cyril's death, combined aspects of Cyril's teaching with "two-nature" language derived from the Antiochene school. The church of Alexandria, being strongly Cyrilline in its understanding of Christ, did not for the most part feel able to accept the Chalcedonian definition, though, as with so many of the doctrinal disputes of the early church, there were political as well as theological issues involved. A certain nationalism played its part, and also resistance to domination by Constantinople, an upstart see (in comparison with the antiquity of Alexandria) and a symbol of Greek domination of the Coptic-speaking Egyptian church. Christians who accepted Chalcedon became known as Melkites — king's men — on account of their adherence to the imperial theology.

The years following the Council of Chalcedon saw rivalry and conflict between the Chalcedonian and non-Chalcedonian Christians of Egypt, and attempts at reuniting them, the *Henoticon* of the Emperor Zeno (482) being one of the most significant. Union was not, however, forthcoming, and relations between the non-Chalcedonian Copts and the Byzantine Melkites worsened as emperors tried to impose their will on Egypt and compel bishops and church leaders to accept the Chalcedonian faith. In this situation of division and rivalry it is not surprising that many Copts welcomed the Arab conquest of Egypt, which meant that the Melkites were no longer backed by the civil power.

Following the Arab conquest of Egypt in the mid-seventh century, the Christians of Egypt found themselves living under Muslim rule. The attitude of the Arab rulers varied towards the Christian population. There were times of tolerance, when Coptic culture flourished. Under some of the Arab rulers the Copts enjoyed considerable prestige and power, particularly under the Fatimid caliphs in the tenth and eleventh centuries (with the exception of the persecuting al–Hakim who destroyed a large number of churches and monasteries between 1012 and 1015). Coptic art and craftsmanship flourished, and the Copts were often employed by the Muslim rulers in the adornment of the great buildings of Cairo. However, almost continually there were pressures of a financial kind through Muslim taxation of the Christians. From the time of the Arab conquest the numbers of Christians in Egypt gradually declined through conversions to Islam, sometimes as a result of direct persecution, more often as a consequence of punitive taxation and land laws. The Copts became a minority in Egypt.

The impact of the Crusades on the Islamic world brought further difficulties for the Christians of the Middle East, the Copts among them. Christian Egypt suffered spasmodically under the various Arab dynasties and under the Ottoman Empire, when Egypt was ruled by the Mamluks as a client dynasty. Sporadic outbreaks of mob violence or official repression could lead to the burning of churches and attacks on Christians. At other times able Copts could rise high in the administration.

Napoleon's invasion of Egypt at the beginning of the nineteenth century marked a new era and an involvement of the Western powers in Egyptian affairs. The nineteenth century also saw the beginning of Protestant missionary activity in Egypt, when an

American Presbyterian mission began work in 1854. The Anglican Church Missionary Society arrived some thirty years later in 1882. Somewhat earlier, as a result of conversions under the influence of Catholic missionaries, a Coptic Catholic Uniate church had come into existence, which was administered by vicars apostolic until Pope Leo XIII set up three dioceses under a Coptic Catholic patriarch in 1895. This Uniate patriarchate did not last long because of schism and dissension among the small number of Uniates, and the jurisdiction of the patriarchate was suspended by Rome and only restored in 1947. It remains a small church (ca. 140,000) but, like the Anglicans and Protestants in Egypt, exercises an influence through its educational and medical work.[5]

The nineteenth century saw the beginning of important developments in the main body of the Coptic Orthodox church, particularly in the fields of education, theological training, publications, and church building and restoration. These were particularly fostered by Patriarch Cyril IV, but there were problems under his successor, Cyril V, a simple monk who found himself in conflict with the growing self-consciousness of the Coptic community expressed in the Community Religious Council (*maglis milli*) inaugurated in 1874. After Cyril's death in 1927 there were continuing difficulties under his three successors. However, contacts had continued to grow with other churches and were marked by important signals such as official representation of the Coptic church at the 1954 assembly of the World Council of Churches. Nevertheless, only in 1956 with the election of Kirollos VI did the church experience firm leadership and spiritual renewal.

Today the Christian population of Egypt is estimated to be some eleven and a half million out of a population of over forty-two million. The majority of that Christian population belongs to the Coptic Orthodox church. In a country often thought of by the outside world as almost entirely Muslim, the presence of the Coptic church is obvious to the visitor. A journey up the Nile is marked by the tall belfries of the Coptic churches emerging from the brilliant green of the fields and the date groves. In Cairo the old district, built on the old Roman fortress of Babylon, contains a cluster of ancient churches, while in another part of the city there is the great cathedral of St Mark which is the patriarchal church of the present Coptic pope, Shenouda III. Pope Shenouda had encouraged a policy of new dioceses to provide better pastoral care and to encourage a close relationship between bishop and people. The bishop is the acknowledged leader in the local Coptic community, and not only does he exercise sacramental and liturgical functions, but his reception room is frequently crowded with people seeking all manner of advice and assistance in their dealings with local government or for relief of various kinds of needs.

Over the last twenty-five years there has been a remarkable revival in the Coptic church which has a significance far beyond Egypt. Part of this revival is an educational and catechetical movement which has links with the Sunday school movement encouraged by Protestant missionaries since the last century. To the surprise of Western visitors with a blinkered perception of the Coptic church as traditional and backward, Christian education is a priority, and tapes and more recently videos are used to the full in Christian instruction. Young Coptic Christians in the towns of the Nile Valley and the Delta go out from the towns to the Christian communities in the villages to assist with instruction. New churches have also been built, a necessity because of the rapidly growing population and the expansion of the towns. From time to time there has been tension between the Christian minority and the Muslim majority, linked in part with the Islamic revival and pressure to introduce Sharia law. It was in this context that Pope Shenouda was confined for a time in the monastery of Deir Amba Bishoi in the Wadi el-Natroun, a situation which produced considerable strain in the church in Egypt and difficulties among the now extensive Coptic diaspora in Europe, Australia, and America.

If catechetical and educational work has played a major part in the Coptic revival, there has also been a growth in social concern. The appointment of bishops for education and social services has been a recognition of this, as in another way has the appointment of a bishop for ecumenical affairs. But the heart of the revival has centred, as the history of the church in Egypt would lead one to expect, on the monasteries. Some thirty years ago there were only the first glimmerings of monastic revival. Since that time the monastic life has flourished in the most remarkable way. Pope Kirollos VI, a notable ascetic, was one of the key figures, as has been his successor, Pope Shenouda, who has combined the spirtuality of the desert with a remarkable gift for communication, giving weekly addresses to thousands in St Mark's cathedral in Cairo, when the Bible is expounded and questions answered. It is said that the cathedral bus stop has now become known simply as "Papa Shenouda."

The monasteries have been physically restored and in many cases extended. There have been a large number of new vocations, particularly among highly educated young Copts, often with degrees in science and technology, who have yet responded to the call to seek God in prayer in the solitude of the desert. Outside Alexandria the monastery of St Menas has been restored. In the Wadi el-Natroun, to the west of the desert road which runs from Cairo to Alexandria, the four monasteries of Deir el-Baramous, Deir el-Surian, Deir Amba Bishoi, and Deir Abu-Maqar (St Macarius) have all grown in size and have expanded into new buildings. At St. Macarius the spiritual father, Abba Matta el-Meskin (Matthew the Poor), the first university graduate to enter a Coptic monastery (in 1947), has inspired what is now a community of some hundred monks. St Macarius has one of the most modern printing presses in Egypt, producing spiritual literature and its own monthly journal *St. Mark*. The desert has been made to blossom through irrigation and the development of a large farm growing fruit, vegetables, and cattle fodder. Monks skilled in agriculture superintend a large herd of cows, which they breed by embryo transplant, and pioneer the cross-breeding of sheep for Egypt's desert conditions. Yet this practical work, which includes the training of peasant workers in new farming techniques, is completely subsidiary to the work of prayer and devotion and theological study, which is at the heart of the monastic life. Further south the two Red Sea monasteries of St Anthony and St Paul flourish, as does St Samuel's to the south of the Faiyyum oasis and Deir el-Muharraq, a pilgrimage centre near Assiut in Middle Egypt. In Upper Egypt, where the only monasteries have for many years been abandoned ones, small communities have come into existence. The religious life for women has also revived, notably in communities in old Cairo and in the community fostered by Bishop Athanasios of Beni Suef. It is from the monasteries that the bishops of the Coptic church are drawn, following the general custom of the Eastern church. To the monasteries come a stream of pilgrims and priests and people seeking spiritual counsel, retreat, and refreshment. The people will say they come "to take a blessing" from the place, whether it be from St Anthony's cave high up on the cliff above his monastery, or the relics of notable desert fathers like Abba John the Short, or one of the three saints Macarii preserved in the monasteries.

For the monks themselves the monastic day begins at three in the morning with an hour's prayer in their cells. At four o'clock the community assembles in church for the morning office, followed by the psalmodia, the songs and chants built around the four "pillars" of the Song of Moses, the Benedicite, Psalm 136, and Psalms 148–150. These vary with the season but always include a great litany of the desert saints and anthems in honour of the Virgin Mary. By seven the community is ready for the day's work as the sun rises over the desert horizon and the bright light penetrates into the shadows of the monastery. If it is a Sunday or festival, the liturgy will follow, preceded by the offering of incense. The liturgy itself will regularly take three hours in a monastery, though it may be shorter in a parish church. In the evening there will be a much shorter evening office.

The traditions of both hermit life and community life are characteristic of Coptic monasticism. The current revival has seen a renewal of both. Vows as the Western church understands them are not a feature of the Coptic monastic tradition, yet there is a real commitment to the monastic life, expressed at profession by the burial service being read over the new monk. He is then given a new name, chosen by the spiritual father of the monastery with reference to the character of the newly professed member of the community. In the traditions of Western monasticism the variety within the monastic life led to the development of different orders and congregations, with the most important distinction being between the active and contemplative life. In Eastern monasticism in general the pattern is more fluid. Within the same community will be found those whose primary work is the reception of guests and the counselling of pilgrims, the running of a printing workshop or desert farm, scholarly research and writing, or a solitary or semi-solitary life of prayer. The desert itself is a pro-portioning place, and the very setting of the monasteries is a constant reminder of the stripping away of the concerns of the world in order that there may be a single-minded devotion to God.

Monks are required to spend some time in the community before they are permitted to embark on the solitary hermit life. This life may be begun within the monastic enclosure, but often involves withdrawal from the monastery to a cave in a cliff (like St Anthony's cave high above his monastery near the Red Sea) or to an ancient tomb hewn out of the rock. A typical hermit's cell in such an ancient tomb might be furnished with a simple reading-desk with the Scriptures and devotional books, a stone slab for sleeping, a table and chair, and a door barring the entrance to protect the hermit from the desert hyenas and other wild beasts. Simple food and a supply of water would come from the monastery.

The call to prayer at the heart of desert monasticism is a call to union with God. That call is also a summons to a concern for the unity of God's people. This can be seen clearly in the strong emphasis that Abba Matta el-Meskin, in his writings, places on the spiritual roots of ecumenism.

> The road to union with God is not a one-way street ending solely with God; on the return journey it leads back to one's neighbour, the stranger, one's enemy, and toward all creation . . . .
>
> Today unity is a subject sought in every field *to prepare* for the union of all with God. This is nothing but an illusion: unity cannot be "temporarily" separated from God so as to be a means of access to God . . . .
>
> Unity without the divine presence is nothing more than an idea, a matter for discussion, or a vain longing. But in the presence of God unity becomes real and visible, overflowing and life-giving, and many live it. When Christ is present in the midst of a community in conflict, controversy cannot keep from ceasing. Every member must begin to fill his eyes and his heart with true unity, and prepare his whole being to receive unity and to give it. [6]

In the early days of desert monasticism monks and communities were drawn from the different nations of the Christian world. There in the desert the unity of the church was realized in the search for God.

At the heart of monastic spirituality is the conviction that Christianity is a divine life. The gift of God is of "his presence and his very Self." Salvation is *theosis*, "deification," as St Athanasius taught in the early centuries. The gift of the Spirit is fellowship, known in "our depths," the "fellowship of love and life with the Father and the Son by the Holy Spirit," a fire "latent in the hearts that know how to kindle it with prayer, humility, and love."

> The Holy Spirit is by nature meek and calm; His voice is never heard and His form never seen except by those that meet with one accord in the intimacy of love and await the promise of the Lord, those that open their hearts and lift their eyes to where Christ sits, demanding the right of children and seeking the face of the Father.

> To these the Spirit manifests Himself as a light for the inner eye and a fire that fills the heart so that every mouth overflows with the praise of God. The young shall see the "Light of the world" in their visions and the old realize Him in their dreams.[7]

The great Byzantine mystic of the turn of the first millennium, St Simeon the New Theologian, taught that the Christian should never receive communion without tears. In the desert monasteries in Egypt today that cleansing gift of tears is a present reality. So too the Jesus Prayer of the Byzantine church is known in the practice of "drawing down the mind into the heart" as verses from psalms, lessons, and psalmodia are used as food for meditation.

A Coptic monk once said to me that growth in prayer might be understood as firstly, the recognition that one's whole life is held in the providence of God, so that nothing that happens in one's life is outside of God's purpose; secondly, the recognition that the saints are our contemporaries; and thirdly, living in that communion and fellowship, the discernment of the divine life within at the very heart of one's own existence. The sense of the saints as contemporaries is a powerful one in the Coptic church. Not only are the desert monasteries holy places, consecrated by the ascetic lives of generations of ''athletes for Christ,'' but they preserve the relics of those who have gone before. The Coptic church is a church of pilgrimage and of festival, and the *mulid* in honour of the saint of a particular church and shrine can attract great crowds. There are numerous *mawalid* in celebration of the coming of the Holy Family to Egypt and their supposed visits to particular towns and villages. There are other popular celebrations in honour of St George or the other warrior-saints, Mercurius, Mina, and Theodore. Frequently there are reports of miracles of healing or strange manifestations of light or an appearance of the saint. The *mawalid* are occasions for baptism and often for circumcision. Some of the shrines and *mawalid* draw both Muslims and Christians, and the festivals attract a large number of side-shows and stalls. At the *mulid* in honour of St Dimiana which is held in May in the delta, between four and six thousand pilgrims gather and camp round the convent for some eight to fifteen days, merchants and magicians alike taking advantage of the large crowd to sell food, drink, clothing, and ornaments, as well as wooden and brass crosses.

Just as the visit of the Holy Family to Egypt plays a central part in popular piety, and is seen as a hallowing of Egypt with their presence, devotion to the Virgin Mary is a significant feature in both popular piety and liturgical prayer. Cyril of Alexandria and many of the early Fathers drew on Old Testament typology in speaking of the Virgin Mother of God. She was seen as the sealed gate of the sanctuary in Ezekiel 44, or was compared with the burning bush on fire with the glory of the Lord yet not consumed. Coptic art shows the Virgin giving suck to the infant Jesus, and some scholars have thought that this may have been influenced by ancient Egyptian depictions of Isis giving suck to her son Horus. There is a sense of wonder in many of the hymns and anthems to the Virgin and the infant Christ. ''He clung to her with his little fingers. He stopped from time to time, and He hung on to the skirts of Mary His Mother — He upon whom the whole creation hangs.'' Any Old Testament figure or incident indicative of the presence of the grace, indwelling, and saving power of God is seized upon as legitimate symbolism to apply to Mary, within whose womb and through whose cooperation the incarnate Lord was born.

> Thou art the censer of pure gold, which was for the coal of burning fire.
> That it was He took from an altar that He might purge sins and remove our transgressions.
> That was God the Word who took flesh in her, he received it to be a sweet savour to God His Father.
> Hail Mary, thou woman whose fruit shall give salvation to the world and to all mankind.
> Thou spotless Dove, in whom there is no blemish . . . .
> Thou pot of gold wherein was the Manna
> Sweet Perfume that mounted up before God Almighty,
> Tent of the Godhead wherein the Only-begotten of the Father hath reposed.
> Thou Ark covered all over with Gold, wherein God the Father sojourned in the Form of His Holy Word.

This devotion to the Virgin provides the context for the appearances of the Virgin at the church of Zeitoun, a suburb of Cairo, not far from the site of the Virgin's tree under which the Holy Family is supposed to have rested on its flight into Egypt. The manifestations began on 2 April 1968. The first to see what appeared to be a woman on the domes of the church were Muslim bus drivers in the depot across the street. From that time until early 1970 there were numerous appearances and associated miracles of healing, conversion, and light phenomena. Bishop Athanasios of Beni Suef gives the following account of what was seen:

> The apparition was seen on various nights . . . . The Virgin Mary sometimes appeared in full form, while on other occasions only the Virgin's bust, surrounded by a glorious halo of shining light appeared. Occasionally the apparition came through an opening in the church's domes, and sometimes it appeared outside the domes. The apparition walked above the altar and bowed before the upper cross of the church. On many

occasions, the apparition faced the people, blessed them, and moved its head as a sign of greeting. The apparition also took the form of a nimbus preceded by a shining white quick-moving white cloud. Sometimes it stayed for periods as long as two and a quarter hours.

Other accounts speak of sheets of light flashing over the church, the fragrance of incense, dove-like appearances, and clouds. Zeitoun is but one of the most important manifestations in recent times of devotion to the Virgin and strange phenomena associated with it. There can be no doubting its impact upon the church both at the time and subsequently.

The Coptic church has a rich cultural tradition, exemplified especially in the ancient churches of old Cairo and in the monasteries and pilgrimage churches of the desert and the Nile Valley. As with all of the Orthodox churches the sanctuary area is divided from the nave of the church by an altar screen, and in many churches this is decorated with inlay work of camel bone or in some instances ivory. Icons are part of this decoration but do not have quite the same prominence as in the Greek and Russian churches. In the older churches the oil lamps which hang before the altar screen are often suspended from ostrich eggs. The worship of the church is liturgical in character, centred on the Divine Liturgy, celebrated according to the ancient liturgy of St Mark. In the parish churches this is largely celebrated in Arabic, but in the monasteries Coptic (which survives to all intents and purposes solely as a liturgical language) is used. The liturgy is sung, with responsorial parts for the priest, the deacons, and the choir, with the people joining in for the well-known anthems and hymns. The only instruments used are cymbals and triangles, which accompany some of the chants with considerable dexterity. Coptic tradition claims that the music of the church has its roots in the music of ancient Egypt — a claim that is not without foundation. What is quite certain is that the long sequences and hymns of the Coptic office and liturgy sung to traditional chant are known by a large percentage of the Coptic community and are an important way in which the faith is handed on. It is not unusual for Coptic taxi drivers to play tapes of monastic chant as they go about their business.

Egypt is the heartland of the Coptic church, but there were early and important links with Ethiopia; the Coptic church in Egypt supplied the bishop for Ethiopia until very recent times. During this century there has grown up a Coptic diaspora, as with the other Oriental churches, with Copts emigrating to various parts of Europe, America, and Australia. In Africa there are two Coptic dioceses in the Sudan and for a time a bishop for African affairs, based in Kenya, Amba Antonious Markos, who developed special links with some of the African independent churches. The Coptic church is also a full member of the World Council of Churches.

Alexandria was a formative influence in the early centuries of the church. Christian monasticism sprang from the deserts of Egypt. Today, the Coptic church, despite political tensions, is alive and vigorous, renewing its educational and monastic traditions alike. This life and vigour is what is most likely to strike the Christian visitor from the West who may frequently be challenged by the faith and spirituality both of young Copts and of the monasteries of the Egyptian desert.

Some Prayers of the Coptic Church

1 Prayer for the rising of the waters of the Nile
Vouchsafe, O Lord, to bless the waters of the river: bring them up after their due measure, after thy grace: gladden the face of the earth: may her furrows be watered, her fruits be multiplied: prepare it for seed and for harvest: provide for our life as may be most expedient according to thy holy and blessed will. Bless the crown of the year with thy goodness for the sake of the poor of thy people, for the sake of the widow and the orphan and the stranger and the sojourner and for the sake of us all who hope in thee and supplicate thy holy name: for the eyes of all wait upon thee, O Lord, for thou givest them their meat in due season. Deal with us after thy great goodness, who givest food to all flesh: fill our hearts with joy and gladness that we also always having sufficiency in all things may abound in every good work.[8]

2 The dismissal at the end of the liturgy
God who art blessed by the seraphim and the cherubim, whom all the angelic hosts glorify and all the choirs of the righteous worship, the foundation and stability of the world, who sustainest

all creation by thine holy godhead and hast made every nature visible and invisible through thine only begotten Son in the Holy Spirit: bless thy servants with all spiritual blessings who have bowed their neck to thee: guard them in the way of righteousness: may they be holy and without blemish: deliver them and preserve them from every operation of the adversary and every power of the devil, open thou their eyes unto the holy mysteries of thy law, fill them with the grace of thine Holy Spirit and keep them without blame from this evil world that now is, comfort them with spiritual and heavenly comfort: may they be accounted worthy of thine inheritance incorruptible to come: by the intercession of the holy glorious ever-virgin *theotokos* S. Mary and the prayers and supplications of the holy archangels Michael and Gabriel, and S. John the forerunner and baptist and martyr, and S. Stephen the deacon and protomartyr, and our holy fathers and apostles, and S. Mark the apostle and evangelist and martyr, and the holy patriarch Severus and our righteous father the great abba Antony and our father abba Paul and the three abbas Macarius and our father abba John and our father abba Pishoi and our Roman fathers and our father abba Moses and the forty-nine martyrs and the holy abba John the black and all the choirs of the saints, through whose prayers and supplications vouchsafe us, O our master, to attain unto a part and a lot with them in the kingdom of heaven: in Christ Jesus our Lord through whom all the glory and all honour and all worship befitteth thee with him and the Holy Spirit the lifegiver and of one substance with thee now and ever and world without end. *Amen* [9]

3 *Salutation to the Blessed Virgin Mary (from the Morning Offering of Incense)*
Hail to thee Mary, the fair dove, which hath borne for us God the Word. We give thee salutation with the Angel Gabriel saying, Hail, thou that art full of grace; the Lord is with thee.

Hail to thee, O Virgin, the very and true Queen; hail glory of our race. Thou hast borne for us Emmanuel.

We pray thee, remember us, O thou our faithful advocate with our Lord Jesus Christ, that He may forgive us our sins.[10]

4 *A Prayer from Mattins (attributed to St Simeon Stylites)*
O God, grant me a prayer without wandering, and recollection

of my thoughts, that I may ask with faith in the promises which Thou hast graciously made unto me.

Grant me clearness in my thoughts and my understanding; let mine heart be enlightened, that mine understanding may know only that which is pure, that I may hear thine everlasting mysteries which Thou hast prepared for mankind in the grace of Thy Christ . . . .

O God grant unto me the love of thine Holy Spirit, to draw mine understanding to love Thee with my whole heart, and my whole soul, and my whole strength, according to that Thou hast said; and love my neighbour even as myself. This is the sum of the law and of the prophets.

Grant unto me to possess my thoughts, that I may not contemplate anything but Thee, may never pray to Thee with the lips only whilst my mind is wandering elsewhere, so that corruption cometh into the core of my heart.

It is written: — The Lord is my light and my salvation.

Yea, O Lord, draw me unto Thyself. Thou art a faithful God and the merciful Father and the Benefactor and the good Teacher.[11]

Endnotes

1 De Lacy O'Leary, *The Saints of Egypt* (London and New York, 1937), p.12; Otto F.A. Meinardus, *Christian Egypt Ancient & Modern* (Cairo, 1977), p. 143.

2 D.J. Chitty, trans., *The Letters of St. Anthony the Great* (Oxford, 1975), p. 21.

3 P. Rousseau, *Pachomius: the making of a community in fourth-century Egypt* (Berkeley, Los Angeles, London, 1985), pp.77-86, 103.

4 Sozomen, *Ecclesiastical History*, VI, xxxi.

5 G. Zananini, *Catholicisme Oriental* (Paris, 1966), pp. 102-7.

6 Matthew the Poor, *The Communion of Love* (Crestwood, New York, 1984), pp. 227-8, 229-30.

7 Matthew the Poor, p. 173.

8 F.E. Brightman, ed., *Liturgies Eastern and Western* (Oxford, 1896), I, 167-8.

9 Brightman, pp. 187-8.

10 John, Marquis of Bute, trans., *The Coptic Morning Service for the Lord's Day* (London, 1908), pp. 24-5.

11 John, Marquis of Bute, pp. 169-170.

For Further Reading
Atiya, A.S., *A History of Eastern Christianity*. London: 1968.
Betts, R.B., *Christians in the Arab East*. London: 1979.
du Bourget P., *Coptic Art*. London. 1971.
Matthew the Poor, *The Communion of Love*. New York: 1984.
Meinardus O.F.M., *Christian Egypt Ancient and Modern*. Cairo: 1977.

The Ethiopians

Colin Battell

The Ethiopian Church, or more properly the Orthodox Tewahedo Church, is the largest of the Oriental Orthodox churches with upwards of 20 million adherents.

The outside world, perhaps because of long periods of isolation endured by Ethiopian Christianity, has often failed to value properly the purity of the doctrine passed down, often by word of mouth. This ignorance of Ethiopia is the reason for our lack of awareness of and surprise at the blending of colour, music, and movement that make up the Ethiopian liturgy. Much of the rooted strength of the Ethiopian church traditions emanates from the firm monastic background supporting it.

Undoubtedly suspicion of foreign Christians existed, and exists, when the foreigners appear to be proselytizing. The Ethiopian church is welcoming to the tactful presence of St Matthew's Anglican parish in Addis Ababa and of the visits by representatives of the Anglican communion. These Anglicans are sensitive to the great riches of the Ethiopian church from which there is so much to learn.

Canon Colin Battell has been rector of St Matthew's for more than eleven years; his ministry and that of his colleague Father Charles Sherlock is directed largely to an African non-Ethiopian congregation, and to liaison with the church of Ethiopia.

D.S.

Historical Background

Until 1974 one of the tourist posters for Ethiopia showed a beautiful Ethiopian processional cross and underneath it the legend: "The oldest Christian Empire in the world." From the fourth century of the Christian era, the history and culture of

Ethiopia have been inextricably linked with the life of the Ethiopian church. Christianity as represented by the Ethiopian Orthodox church was the official religion of the country and its rulers, who in their mountain stronghold preserved an island of Christian faith amidst an Islamic sea. Because of its geographical isolation from other Christians, the Ethiopian church has preserved a number of unique features and has developed its own distinctive traditions. With at least 20 million followers, it remains the largest of the Oriental churches in the world today.

The conversion of the first Ethiopian Christian is recorded in the Acts of the Apostles when the apostle Philip met and converted a court official who was returning home from a visit to Jerusalem (Acts 8: 26–40). Nothing is known of what became of him. There is also a tradition that St Matthew was sent as an apostle and evangelist to Ethiopia, but there is no contemporary historical evidence.

The history of Christianity in Ethiopia really begins in the fourth century. The Roman historian Rufinus tells the story of St Frumentius and his companion Aedesius, two boys from the Roman Empire, who were shipwrecked on the Ethiopian coast and became attached to the royal court at Axum, the ancient capital of Ethiopia. St Frumentius, who is known in Ethiopia as Abba Selama (Father of Peace) and Kassate Berhan (Revealer of Light), wielded considerable political influence, especially during a period when he assisted the king's mother, who was acting as a regent, in governing the country. During that time, he encouraged Christian Roman merchants to build places of worship and promoted them to positions of importance. Later St Frumentius was reluctantly allowed to leave, and he came to Alexandria where he informed St Athanasius, the newly appointed bishop, that there were now Christians in Ethiopia who needed a bishop to care for them spiritually. St Athanasius decided to consecrate St Frumentius himself and sent him back to serve in Ethiopia.

The story of Rufinus ends at this point, but it is known from coins, inscriptions, and other evidence that King Ezana was converted to Christianity in the first quarter of the fourth century, and from that time the rulers of Ethiopia have been Christians.

Thus, unlike in the Roman Empire where, broadly speaking, Christianity began with the conversion of the lower elements of society and gradually worked its way to the ruling classes and eventually the emperor, in Ethiopia, Christianity began with the conversion of the emperor and the royal court, and this slowly led to the conversion of other sections of society. Christianity was, therefore, an integral part of the national life culturally, politically, and socially from an early period, and the history of the government of the country has until very recent times been linked with the life of the church.

The ancient empire, centred on Axum, had regular contacts with the Roman and Byzantine Empires until the Muslim conquests made it increasingly isolated from the rest of the Christian world. However, the church of Alexandria was always regarded as the mother church of Ethiopia; and indeed there were no Ethiopian bishops until the twentieth century, the sole member of the episcopate being a Copt sent from Egypt by the pope of Alexandria. This arrangment had a number of disadvantages. Continuity was sometimes difficult, and the bishop was isolated from his people by ignorance of their language. In this situation, the Ethiopian head of the clergy, called the *Echege*, from the fifteenth century the head of the monastery of Debre Libanos in Shewa, exercised considerable power and influence at the royal court. Ethiopian bishops were finally appointed in 1929 when four priests were consecrated to the episcopate. Following lengthy negotiations with the Coptic church, the autonomy of the Ethiopian church was established in 1957 and patriarchial status was granted to the head of the Ethiopian church. The present patriarch, Abuna Tekle Haimanot, is thus only the third Ethiopian patriarch.

It ought perhaps to be noted here that Ethiopian Christians should not be called Copts, as sometimes erroneously happens, since clearly they are not Egyptians and the official title of the church is the Ethiopian Orthodox Tewahido (United Nature) Church.

The church today is governed by the Holy Episcopal Synod, but according to the agreement made with the Coptic church, its dogma can only be changed in consultation with the church of Alexandria and the other Oriental churches.

The close links with Egypt ensured that the Ethiopian church joined the other Oriental churches in rejecting the teaching of the

Council of Chalcedon concerning the nature of Christ. The position of the Ethiopian church in this respect is well summarized by Professor V.C. Samuel.

> Many prayers in the Liturgy show that the manhood of Christ was absolutely real and perfect. But everywhere the emphasis is on the Unity of Jesus Christ . . . . The two natures of Godhead and manhood which came into union in Him continue in the One Christ, each in its absolute integrity and perfection with its respective properties, without change or division . . . .
>
> The Church of Ethiopia, with the other Oriental Orthodox churches has refused to accept the Chalcedonian definition of the faith with the affirmation that Christ is made known in two natures. If by this expression, churches which accept the definition mean only that Godhead and manhood continue in the one Christ, dynamically, this is the teaching of the Ethiopian Orthodox Church. On the other hand, if the expression is taken in the sense that Godhead and manhood continue in Christ only in a state of moral union, there is a basic difference on this issue between the churches of the Chalcedonian tradition and the Ethiopian Church which should be noted.[1]

In the fifth century, the coming of the "Nine Saints," as they are called, from Syria helped to establish and extend Christianity within the country. They translated the Bible into Ge'ez, the ancient language of Ethiopia, often called Ethiopic, using a Syrio-Greek text. They also translated a number of patristic writings as well. The Ethiopian canon of scripture contains a number of extra books in both the Old and New Testaments; and the greater part of the complete books of Enoch, Jubilees, and the Ascension of Isaiah are now extant only in their Ethiopic forms.

It is difficult to give accurate figures concerning the numbers of Christians in Ethiopia at the present time. An official census in 1984 discovered that the population of the country was 42 million as against the previous estimate of 32 million.

There are probably about 20 million Christians with a slightly smaller number of Muslims, the rest being animists. Muslims have occupied the lowlands and have not been so important politically as their numbers might suggest. A Christian king of Ethiopia in the time of Mohammed allowed Muslim refugees from Arabia to settle peacefully in Ethiopia, but there have sometimes been periods of serious conflict between Muslims and the Christian highland rulers.

If in the words of Khomiakov, Orthodoxy has until recent times been "a new and unknown world" for Western Christians, this is certainly true of their knowledge of the Ethiopian church. Gibbon's famous sentence, "Encompassed on all sides by the enemies of their religion, the Ethiopians slept near a thousand years forgetful of the world by whom they were forgotten," has been a factor in forming Western estimates of Ethiopian Christianity. The sentence needs some qualification; but it effectively makes the point that the Ethiopian church has often been the subject of Western ignorance and underestimation.

The Ethiopian church is, in fact, a very "popular" church, in the best sense of the word, exercising considerable influence over the lives of its followers. People flock to church in Ethiopia in numbers that can scarcely be imagined in many Western countries. On major festivals which are celebrated monthly rather than annually, the faithful attend church in thousands. The celebration of the feast of St Gabriel, in recent times a very popular saint, at the pilgrimage at Kulubi in south eastern Ethiopia, attracts in excess of 100,000 worshippers. Devotion to the Virgin Mary, the archangels, St George the patron of Ethiopia, and many other saints is also vigorous and forms an essential part of Ethiopian piety. Thus, the communion of saints is a reality for Ethiopian Christians in a very intense and meaningful way.

Until 1974, the church was an established church and received considerable imperial patronage and support. In many ways it was controlled by the emperor, and appointments of bishops and other senior clergy were an imperial prerogative. In return, many ecclesiastics exercised considerable influence in the councils of state. The church owned vast areas of land (perhaps as much as fifteen per cent of the total) and was second only to the crown as a landowner. It also owned real estate which produced a large income in rent. (It is said, for example, that church property in Addis Ababa alone produced the equivalent of about six million dollars U.S. annually.)

The revolution of 1974 brought to an end the imperial dynasty and separated church from state. It also nationalized all land, the church's chief source of wealth, and a great deal of property. The church, thus, overnight lost most of its revenue. By way of compensation the government still pays the church the equivalent of about two million U.S. per year, but this is only a fraction of its previous income.

The church is now officially responsible for its own appointments and, in fact, all except one of the bishops, contrary to previous practice, have been retired and replaced. In 1976 a new patriarch, Abuna Tekle Haimanot, was elected to replace Abuna Tewofilos, who had been jailed earlier in the year.

Thus, the Ethiopian church has been faced during the last twelve years with the difficult task of adjusting from being the established church to being the church in a country whose political system is guided by the principles of Marxism-Leninism. The government has not formally issued directives concerning its attitude to religion, but the new constitution guarantees freedom of religion, provided it does not operate in ways that jeopardize the aims of the revolution. The government guarantees freedom of religious practice, and went out of its way to ensure that religious leaders should be seen to be taking part in the drafting of the constitution promulgated prior to the establishment of a People's Democratic Republic in September 1986.

In practice, the pattern seems to be very similar to the one that has emerged in many other communist countries where the predominant Christian church was Orthodox. The Orthodox church has stressed that it is not subject to persecution and has been anxious to avoid any suggestion of confrontation with the state. The administrator of the church, a government appointee, ensures that no conflict arises in church-state relations. In return, no Orthodox churches have been closed and, indeed, a number of sumptuous new churches have been built in the capital and elsewhere by the donations of the faithful.

Ethiopian Churches

It is estimated that in Ethiopia there are over 15,000 churches of varying size and grandeur. The most famous and amazing churches were built at Lalibella in the twelfth and thirteenth centuries by rulers of the Zagwe dynasty. These enormous monolithic constructions are carved out of the solid rock and are rightly considered among the wonders of the world. Other such rock churches exist, especially in the north of the country, and are fine repositories of Ethiopian art, which is almost entirely religious. In fact, Ethiopian art is extremely distinctive and sophisticated, and represents a unique combination of Oriental and Byzantine styles. Priests carry intricate hand crosses of brass, silver, or wood with which they bless the faithful as they meet them, and processional crosses of great beauty are found in many of the churches.

In the north of the country, churches are usually of the basilica type and are built of stone, while further south, in imitation of the domestic architecture, they are often round with roofs of thatch or, more recently, corrugated iron.

Churches are often set on a hill surrounded by trees and a walled compound. The whole compound is regarded as part of the church, and those who have committed certain sins pray outside the church building. The faithful kiss the doorposts of the church and prostrate themselves before removing their shoes and entering the church. Churches are often richly decorated with scenes from the Bible and lives of the saints, especially the Virgin, the apostles, and St George. At the east end of the church compound is the Bethlehem (House of Bread), a small building where the sacramental bread and wine are prepared by the deacons.

All Ethiopian churches have three distinct sections, which in round churches form concentric circles. In the innermost circle, the *Meqdas* (Holy of Holies), is the altar on which rests the *tabot* or ark of the covenant, which is the mark of the holiness of a church. Ethiopian monarchs traced their dynasty to the union of King Solomon and the Queen of Sheba which led to the birth of Menelik I. According to the Ethiopian tradition, the original Ark of the Covenant on which the Ten Commandments had been inscribed by God for Moses was brought to Axum, the ancient capital of Ethiopia, where it is still to be found today. All other churches contain one or more *tabots* dedicated to God or his saints and, indeed, a building is no longer regarded as consecrated if there is no *tabot* present in it. These *tabots* are treated with the greatest possible reverence. On major festivals they are taken out of the church on the heads of the priests in solemn procession round the church, and are venerated by the faithful as a sacramental sign of God's presence among his people.

The *tabot* is an example of Jewish influence on the Orthodox church in Ethiopia. The Orthodox tradition traces this influence to pre-Christian times, though its exact provenance is uncertain. Thus, circumcision is practised in Ethiopia, and a distinction is made between clean and unclean meats, following the Mosaic prohibition in Leviticus. Ethiopian Christians argue that these rules still apply to them because the original converts to Christianity were converts not from paganism but from Judaism. Boys are normally baptized 40 days after birth and girls after 80 days, following the Jewish rules concerning the presentation of infants in the temple, and the Sabbath is observed as well as Sunday.

The second major division within the church is the *Qeddist* where the communicants congregate, the men divided from the women. Only those who have been to confession, have fasted, and are fully prepared are permitted to receive communion and, in practice, communicants are usually very young or old people. Those who have not been married in church are not allowed to communicate. Since relatively few people marry in this way, most of the faithful are permanently excommunicated.

The third of the three divisions is the *Qene Mahlet* (Place of Song) which itself is divided into three parts. The western part is occupied by the *debteras*. These are the church singers, but singing is not their only role. They form a kind of order between the clergy and the laity which has no exact parallel in other churches. Often they are steeped in church learning and are also involved in treating the sick with herbal remedies. In the church they lead the singing to the accompaniment of drums and sometimes other musical instruments. Drums are not, however, used during fasting seasons. The *debteras* also perform a kind of liturgical dance with prayer sticks *(maqomiya)* and *sistra*. These prayer sticks are also used as a means of support by the elderly and important members of the congregation. The services are often very long, and there are no seats except in a few modern city churches. The specially devout do not use prayer sticks, while the really pious may pray standing on one leg only, following the practice of St

Tekle Haimanot, who prayed in this way for many years. The other two parts of the *Qene Mahlet* are used by men and women who have their respective entrances into the church.

The Liturgy

The liturgy (*Qidasse*) is celebrated in the Holy of Holies, which only the priests and deacons may enter. It is celebrated early in the morning except on fast days, when it is at midday. A minimum of two priests and three deacons is necessary for the celebration of the liturgy. For this reason the clergy are very numerous indeed, perhaps over 200,000 in the country as a whole. Large churches have many clergy who serve a course of duty on a rota basis. Deacons are often young boys, and priests must choose whether they wish to marry before being ordained, as in other Orthodox churches.

To understand the ethos of the Ethiopian church, it is necessary to participate in its worship, which is at the centre of its life and activity. The liturgy of the Ethiopian church is unique in that it has no less than fourteen anaphoras (eucharistic prayers) which are used on various occasions. These are in Ge'ez, the ancient Ethiopian language, which is still the official language of the church. Ge'ez is closer to Tigrinya and Tigre, languages of northern Ethiopia, than to modern Amharic, the official language of Ethiopia today, and is not well known outside clerical and scholarly circles. Amharic is increasingly used in parts of the liturgy, and sermons are preached in Amharic where that is the language of the people. In fact, the laity know the shape and form of the liturgy well and join in the responses enthusiastically. Ge'ez may, perhaps, be compared with the use of Latin in the Roman Catholic church before the Second Vatican Council. It is felt by some that the use of Ge'ez, a language no longer spoken, helps to preserve doctrinal purity.

The exact origin of the eucharistic prayers is unknown. They first appear in manuscripts of the fifteenth century but were doubtless composed very much earlier. Scholars at one time assumed that all or most of these anaphoras were translations of foreign liturgies but recent studies such as those of Ernst Hammerschmidt have demonstrated that many of the anaphoras are genuine creations of Ethiopian literature evincing theological thought and liturgical poetry of a high order.[2]

The priests and deacons wear highly colourful vestments, and the more wealthy churches possess vast quantities of gorgeous velvet vestments with rich embroidery in gold and silver.

Umbrellas are used not only as a shade from sun or rain but also as a mark of honour and distinction, and are used in all churches ceremonially. Often highly decorated, they are held over officiating clergy and church dignitaries at various points in the liturgy. It is a pious custom for the faithful to donate such umbrellas to a church as thank offerings, and most churches receive them in large numbers.

Monasticism

Monasticism has played an important part in the life of the church, and bishops are always chosen from among the monks. The monasteries in Ethiopia have been important centres of culture and learning. Even today the larger monasteries have several hundred monks attached to them. Ethiopian monastic rules are based on the rule of St Pachomius. For the most part monks live an idiorhythmic monastic life; many also live an eremitic life. Some appear outside churches at the greater festivals as freelance preachers dressed in animal skins not unlike latter-day John the Baptists. Monasteries are often in inaccessible places of astonishing grandeur and natural beauty. The monastery of Debre Damo in northern Ethiopia is still only accessible by rope.

Among the most venerated of Ethiopian monks is St Tekle Haimanot, who lived in a cave at Debre Libanos and founded the monastery there. Extracts from the story of his life and miracles, beautifully illustrated from an eighteenth-century manuscript, have recently been published in English.

Fasting

Fasting is observed by Ethiopian Christians with a seriousness that makes the practice of most Western Christians look slack in the extreme. The Fetha Negest, or Law of the Kings, an ancient secular and ecclesiastical book of laws, defines fasting as follows:

Fasting is abstinence from food and is observed by men at certain times determined by law to attain forgiveness of sins and reward, obeying the one who fixed the law. Fasting (also) serves to weaken the force of concupiscence so that (the body) may obey the rational soul.[3]

Many Ethiopian Christians are deeply shocked by the neglect of fasting by Western Christians, since it seems to indicate a lack of seriousness in those who are following the way of Christ. Our Lord fasted often and made his followers do the same. It is, therefore, an essential part of the discipline of the Christian life.

Fasting is strictly observed by all the faithful, the clergy observing as many as 256 fast days in the year while the laity observe about 180 days a year. There are seven official fasting periods:

1　All Wednesdays and Fridays, except during the 50 days of Easter.
2　The Lenten fast (56 days).
3　The fast of Nineveh (3 days shortly before Lent).
4　The vigils of Christmas and Epiphany.
5　The fast of the apostles (between 14 and 44 days before the feast of SS Peter and Paul; the precise length of this fast depends on the date of Easter).
6　The fast of the prophets (43 days).
7　The fast of the Assumption (15 days in August before the feast of the Passing Away of the Mother of God).

The fasts of the apostles and the prophets are only compulsory for clergy, though many of the devout laity undertake them as well. Fasting may be undertaken as a penance in addition to the corporate fasts of the church and is often prescribed by confessors, who care for families and individuals spiritually. The church lays down precise rules for the observance of fast days. They include abstention from all meat and animal products (butter, milk, eggs, etc.) and from all food until the end of the liturgy in the early afternoon. All are expected to fast except the very young, the sick, and the very old; failure to observe the fasts still leads to social ostracism in many rural areas. It is interesting to observe that even those whose adherence to the church may in other ways be fairly nominal can still often be found rigorously keeping the fasts. In Holy Week many people fast completely from food and drink from Good Friday until after the liturgy on Easter Day, when the fast is broken in the early morning following the completion of the liturgy at about 3 am.

Church Festivals

Church festivals also play an important part in the life of Ethiopian Christians and, since major festivals are celebrated each month, time is reckoned in this way especially in country areas. Thus, asked what day of the month it is, many people reply, St Mary's Day, rather than the 21st.

The Ethiopian church follows the Coptic calendar of twelve months of thirty days and one of five or six (hence the celebrated tourist advertising feature in Ethiopia, "Thirteen months of sunshine"). There is also a difference of seven or eight years between the Western and Ethiopian calendars, and New Year's Day is the eleventh of September. Each year is named after one of the evangelists in a four-year cycle.

Two major festivals which are celebrated in a distinctive way are Timqat (Baptism or Epiphany) and Mesqel (The Finding of the True Cross). As in other Orthodox churches, Epiphany celebrates the revelation of the divinity of Jesus at his Baptism and is essentially a celebration of the Incarnation, although Christmas is also observed, on 7 January. At Timqat, the *tabots* are carried from the church in procession to a place where there is water. There they stay overnight in tents. The next morning the waters are blessed and the *tabots* return to their churches. This is a festival of great rejoicing and is a major public holiday.

Mesqel, which celebrates the finding of the True Cross by the Empress Helena, falls at the end of September. This is marked by the lighting of bonfires throughout the land, since according to tradition the empress was led to excavate the place where the cross was buried by a miraculous smoke which came out of the ground. In the capital, the mayor of Addis Ababa lights the bonfire in the presence of the patriarch in Revolution Square (formerly Mesqel Square) together with tens of thousands of the faithful, beneath massive portraits of Marx, Engels, and Lenin. (The celebration has been moved to another site still in the centre of town.)

Education

It is barely an exaggeration to say that until the twentieth century the church was entirely responsible for education in the country. Still today many churches have schools attached to them giving education at various levels. The church has its own system of education from the teaching of the *fidel* (the letters of the Ge'ez alphabet, also used for the writing of all languages in Ethiopia) to the very highest levels of theological thought. Many of the schools simply give instruction in reading, poetry, church music, and scripture while others combine modern and traditional education. According to the traditional system, reading and writing were usually seen as separate skills.

Education in church schools begins with the learning of the *fidel*, the characters of the Ge'ez alphabet. Next, the first letter of St John is read in Ge'ez followed by other biblical writings, with special emphasis on the psalms which may be learnt by heart even in their entirety. In fact, great emphasis is placed on the learning of passages of scripture and other Christian writings so that they may be recited from memory.

Beyond this elementary education, there are higher forms of education which are pursued by some students. They sometimes travel vast distances in order to attach themselves to a distinguished teacher. The Qidasse Bet (School of Liturgy) trains priests in the celebration of the liturgy, while the Zema Bet (Music School) gives lessons in the music of the Ethiopian church. Ethiopian music is very distinctive and has been handed down from the time of St Yared, the founder of Ethiopian church music who lived in the sixth century. The music when well performed can be hauntingly beautiful in its cumulative effect, and competent singers are greatly admired. There is a method of writing the music above the text by use of diacritic marks, but singing is normally performed without books of any kind.

The Qene Bet (Poetry School) composes hymns for use in the liturgy and on special occasions. These poems have levels known as "wax and gold," the wax being the obvious surface meaning, the gold being the profounder meaning which may not be immediately apparent. Qene has to be sung, and requires tremendous skill and a very considerable degree of creativity. Indeed, Qene experts are held in high honour for their intellectual brilliance by Ethiopians, who are greatly interested in and impressed by a sophisticated use of language. The highest form of church education is the Metshaf Bet (School of Commentaries) in which the student has to learn by heart commentaries on the scriptures and other religious writings. To become an expert in this branch of learning requires very many years of patient study and labour. Those advanced in it are regarded as church scholars. Again, stress is placed on memorizing, since it is only in recent times that the ability to read and write has become at all widespread. Moreover, it is felt that learning by heart prevents the student from involving himself in useless speculations and also avoids his approaching the sacred texts in a critical spirit. The church is well aware of the need for future leaders to be trained in modern as well as traditional education. However, it is easy for Western observers to underestimate the importance and strength of the traditional church education, which in its most advanced form requires prodigious intellectual skill.

A theological college operated as part of the University of Addis Ababa until 1974. This college trained people to a high level by way of a degree course, but unfortunately virtually no students went to serve the church from it. Instead they joined the government bureaucracy like most other graduates. The church lost the buildings of this college to the university following the revolution of 1974. More recently a theological college has been opened in Kolfe in the west of the capital and is offering a much more basic three-to-four year course to men already ordained. The education of the clergy is recognized as a great need within the church. Many of the clergy are peasant farmers and have little theological formation apart from a knowledge of the liturgy. One of the programs sponsored by the World Council of Churches has been a clergy training program, and among these the one at Zwai, founded by Abuna Gorgorios, archbishop of Shewa, is well known as giving a broad education to members of the clergy.

The church also has its own printing press and publishing house which publishes religious works in Amharic and Ge'ez, and a newspaper and other journals in Amharic.

Prayer

The faithful are urged to devote considerable time and effort to prayer, and many Ethiopians, who for the most part are a deeply religious people, do so. The *Fetha Negest* reminds the faithful that prayer is man's way of communicating with God. The following precepts are laid down:

> Firstly he should stand up as enjoined in the words of the Lord. "When you rise up for prayer you shall stand up." Secondly, he should gird himself with a girdle as the Lord said, "Let your loins be girded." Thirdly, he should turn towards the East, for that is the direction from which Christ will appear in His second coming. Fourthly, he should make the sign of the cross from the forehead downward and from left to right. Fifthly, he should recite the prayer in fear and trembling. Sixthly, he should kneel down and prostrate himself since the Gospel tells us that on the night of His passion, our Lord prayed prostrating himself and kneeling.[4]

Prostration in fact plays a large part in Ethiopian worship, and on Good Friday the faithful spend the whole day in church performing the act of prostration many hundreds of times, to the limits of their physical strength.

Ethiopian Christians are urged to pray seven times a day after the manner of King David, and often people go to pray in church outside of service times. The following is an example of an Ethiopian prayer of hope:

> My Lord and God Jesus Christ, Son of the Living God, I ask and beseech Thee to keep my soul and body in Thy fear; and cut me not down like a worthless tree which has no fruit, and take me not suddenly out of this world, but wait and be patient with me, that I may repent and bring unto Thee the fruit of repentance. Should the earth by reason of the mulitude of my

sins repair to Thee for my doom, say to it, "Have patience." Should the angels have recourse to Thee at the multitude of my errors, say to them, "Have patience."

O loving Jesus, my sin is not a burden too heavy for Thee to bear. Sprinkle Thy blood on me and cleanse me, change my death into life, my darkness into light, my weakness into strength; let not my life be beneath Thy regard: for Thou art He who desirest not the death of a sinner. Have patience with me in the multitude of Thy mercies, and bring me to Thyself in the multitude of Thy compassions, and forgive my sins and errors, and blot out all mine offences, and cause me to receive a recompense with those who have been well pleasing to Thee. For Thine is the power and the Kingdom, and to Thee be praise, world without end. Amen. [5]

Church Aid and Development

The Orthodox church ministers to the whole man — body, mind, and spirit — so it shows concern for its members who may be suffering physically as well as spiritually. The Development and Inter Church Aid Department (DICAD) of the patriarchate has taken a very active role in ministering to those who suffered in the recent terrible famine which affected almost a quarter of the population. With grants from the World Council of Churches and from other sources as well as with contributions from the faithful, it has operated feeding programs, provided medical care, and set up development programs to enable farmers to become self-sufficient. The Child Care Council also runs a number of orphanages for some 8,000 children and is looking after more since the recent crisis.

Ethiopian Contacts with Other Countries

Today, the Ethiopian church has fourteen dioceses within Ethiopia corresponding to the administrative regions, each with its own archbishop. He is a member of the Holy Episcopal Synod which governs the church and is responsible for the work of the church in his diocese. His see is in the provincial capital, and under his supervision are departments of missions, youth, education, and the church treasury.

Although it has often been isolated from contact with the outside world, Ethiopia has had a much longer history of contact with foreign parts than many other African regions. Many Ethiopian ecclesiastics, in the steps of the first Ethiopian convert to Christianity, make their way to Jerusalem, where an Ethiopian church has been in existence since the late twelfth century. Part of the church of the Holy Sepulchre in Jerusalem is occupied by Ethiopian monks, and over three hundred pilgrims go to the Holy City each year for the celebration of Easter through the Jerusalem Memorial of Ethiopian Believers, an independent Orthodox organization, which exists to assist the work of the Ethiopian church in Jerusalem as well as undertaking spiritual and charitable work in Ethiopia itself.

Recent years have seen a concern for Ethiopian Christians living outside the country and for the evangelization of others too, although the Ethiopian church has few non-Ethiopian members except in the West Indies. Bishops have been appointed for Sudan and Djibouti, and the Western Hemisphere, which is the diocese which covers the work of the Ethiopian church in North America, the West Indies, and Europe. One of the practical ways in which Anglicans may be able to assist the Ethiopian church abroad is by providing church buildings to enable Ethiopians to worship according to their tradition. This has already happened in some places.

There is a long tradition of Ethiopians going abroad for theological study to Greece, Russia, and Eastern Europe as well as to non-Orthodox countries. A further way of practical cooperation could be through the provision of scholarships to enable more students to do this. Similarly, Anglican students need to be encouraged to take an interest in, and spend time studying and learning from, the Ethiopian tradition. Too often in the past this has been the concern of a few missionaries and other individuals who have become deeply involved and committed to supporting the work of a church whose heroic witness, often against astounding odds, remains unsung and unknown.

Relations with Other Churches

Of the Christians in Ethiopia about 90 per cent belong to the Ethiopian Orthodox church. This needs always to be remembered when contemplating the situation of Christians in Ethiopia. Often in its history, the Ethiopian church has been isolated from contact with other Christians, and such contacts as it has had have not always been happy. Attempts by Catholics to convert Ethiopian rulers met with fierce opposition from the Orthodox clergy and faithful, and were never successful except for the briefest periods. The Italian fascist invasion and occupation of Ethiopia (1936-1941) was also resisted by the Orthodox church, and a number of bishops and clergy were among the martyred patriots.

Protestants arrived in the nineteenth century (at the same time as the Anglican Bishop Samuel Gobat) often with the intention of working with the indigenous church, but soon set up their own churches. The Emperor Haile Selassie (might of the Trinity), following the example of other recent emperors, allowed missionaries into the country because of their technical skills and medical and educational work, but they were not permitted to work in predominantly Orthodox areas. For that purpose Addis Ababa was declared an open area where foreign missions might be allowed to establish headquarters and operate. Often the foreign Protestant missions, now sometimes described as "newcomers" or "Western Christians," have been and still are heavily dependent on financial aid from outside. In practice, they represent Western values and for this reason have sometimes come into conflict with the present government. It should, however, always be remembered that non-Orthodox Christians in Ethiopia represent a very small percentage of the Christian population.

The Anglican church in Ethiopia has followed a different policy from other churches and has not made any attempt to proselytize among Orthodox Christians. Indeed, it is committed to supporting and working to strengthen the life of the ancient and indigenous church and, thus, there are no Ethiopian Anglicans.

Such Anglican missions as have worked in the country in recent times, the Bible Churchmen's Missionary Society and the Church's Ministry among the Jews, have worked with the permission of, and in close cooperation with, the Orthodox church. The latter mission was working among the Felashas, a tribe of Ethiopian Jews in Northwest Ethiopia, and any converts they made were baptized into the Ethiopian Orthodox church. Missionaries from these societies were almost entirely from the

evangelical wing of the Anglican church and had reservations
about some aspects of the Orthodox tradition. But many of them
grew to value and love the Ethiopian church and gave it
unstinting service. Missionaries such as David Stokes, Roger
Cowley, Michael Blair, and Eric Payne are remembered with great
affection and exercised considerable influence on those to whom
they ministered, some of whom occupy senior positions within
the church today.

Both these missions left in the mid 1970s, and the only remaining Anglican presence is an expatriate congregation at St Matthew's, Addis Ababa. The clergy of the Anglican chaplaincy work
to maintain, and are committed to developing, good relations with
the Orthodox church. They are currently engaged in an
orphanage program for drought victims linked to various parishes
where the children are brought up as Orthodox Christians.

In setting up an expatriate chaplaincy great care was taken not
to appear to be trying to proselytize Orthodox Christians. Canon
Austin Mathew who was chaplain 1928 – 54 and stayed on after
his retirement until his death in 1967, played a leading part in
producing a modern Amharic version of the Bible and was wholly
committed to supporting the work of the Ethiopian Orthodox
church. He was very critical of those missionaries who failed to
perceive the glories and riches of the Orthodox tradition and were
only concerned to point out its weaknesses. Writing, in the early
1940s, to the Society for the Propagation of the Gospel, who had
sent him to Ethiopia, he asserted:

> The criticisms of the Abyssinian Church which I have read in
> books seem to me to be the superficial comments anyone might
> make. I have not seen any attempt at sympathy and under-
> standing. I am not prepared with the partial evidence before
> me to agree with the other missionaries that the church is dead
> and that the only thing to do is to replace it with purer forms
> of Christianity. I am not ready to give up hope of a revival
> which will enable it to undertake its own missionary work.[6]

The Ethiopian Orthodox church was a founder member of the
World Council of Churches and has valued the material aid and
Christian fellowship it has received from it. If at times it seems

suspicious of the motives of other churches, this can often be explained by its experience of foreign missionaries who have been unsympathetic to the Orthodox tradition and who have been openly keen to proselytize and compete with it.

The Ethiopian Orthodox church is deeply rooted in the culture of its people. Even at times when the hierarchy has been weak or controlled by the state, it has given heroic witness to the truth of the Christian faith through the lives of countless millions of faithful people. Ethiopia is one of the poorest countries in the world and through civil unrest and natural disasters has faced grave difficulties in recent years. Ethiopians are justly proud of their Christian culture and are highly conscious that they are the heirs of a noble tradition. In spite of all its problems, Christians of the Orthodox Tewahedo church have never doubted that Ethiopia will still "hasten to stretch out her hands unto God."[7]

Endnotes

1 V.C. Samuel, "The Faith of the Church," in *The Church of Ethiopia, A Panorama of History and Spiritual Life*, ed. Sergew Hable Selassie (Addis Ababa: Ethiopian Orthodox Church, 1970) p. 51.
2 Admasu Amare and Belaynesh Michael, "The Role of the Church in Literature and Art," Selassie, p. 79.
3 *The Fetha Negest, the Law of the Kings*, trans. Abba Paulos Tzadua (Addis Ababa University, 1968) p. 93.
4 *The Fetha Negest*, ch. 14.
5 Cited in Douglas O'Hanlon, "Features of the Abyssinian Church," in Rodwell, *Ethiopic Liturgies and Hymns* (SPCK, 1946).
6 A.F. Mathew, Unpublished Papers in the Archives of the United Society for the Propagation of the Gospel, London.
7 Psalm 68:31.

The Syrians of Syria and South India

William H. Taylor

Here we have a brief and well-balanced introduction to Syrian Orthodoxy in the Middle East and in South India. The Syrian Orthodox church has been in contact with the Church of England since the thirties of the last century; this story is as instructive of well-meaning Anglican initiatives as of the short sightedness to which we are prone.

We may well call this ancient church that of the West Syrians in order to distinguish it from the church of the East Syrians, who are members the Assyrian Church of the East; the history of the one complements and needs to be read alongside the other.

A modern chapter to all of this is the pan-Anglican ecumenical outreach to these churches in their homelands and in their diaspora, referred to in other parts of our study. This is evidenced here by the strong relationships which have been cultivated by Father William Taylor among the Suriani (West Syrians) of south-eastern Turkey as well as in England and northern Europe.

I have myself paid three visits of friendship on behalf of the Anglican communion to the Syrian patriarchate in Damascus; 1984 and again in 1987 and 1988; and to the catholicosate of the Syrian church in Kerala in 1984; both these branches of the Syrian Orthodox church intend to send official observers to the Lambeth Conference of 1988.

William Taylor is an Anglican priest, the archbishop of Canterbury's advisor on Orthodox affairs. He is on the staff of a central London church. A Syriac speaker, he has lived with the Syrian Orthodox in eastern Turkey; he wrote his doctoral thesis on the relationship between Anglicans and Syrians, 1874-1928. He is Syrian Orthodox consultant to the Middle Eastern Regional Committee of the World Council of Churches.

H.H.

Introduction

A minority sometimes welcome, sometimes not, is often wounded. It is drawn to its own community, where corporate strength is a precious resource. Survival requires special skill, special faith; the community is constantly winnowed by the loss of those without courage and those too selfish to persevere. So the little band is purged and matured, until it has a unique and precious contribution to make to the very society which is at the same time its scourge and its nourishment.[1]

The history of the Syrian Orthodox church, either in the Middle East or in India, is the history of a minority. Minorities are often overlooked, and the history of the Syrian Orthodox church is little known in the West; few Western scholars have undertaken a history of that church, especially in the modern period. I do not claim to be undertaking such a major and long-term endeavour, but merely offer some reflections on the history of Syrian Orthodoxy in relation to Anglicanism. My reflections are based on the experience of the living tradition and the friendship and encouragement I have received from my Syrian Orthodox friends, both in the Middle East (especially Turkey) and in India; and more specifically, on the results of a more detailed study of Syrian Orthodox-Anglican relations from the early nineteenth to the mid-twentieth centuries.

Historical Perspective: The Middle East

Antioch and Edessa — The Apostolic and Patristic Period

The origins of Syrian Orthodoxy in the Middle East represent the origins of the Apostolic church. We read in Acts 11:26 that it was in the city of Antioch "that the disciples were for the first time called Christians." The disciples of Christ were to be found in Antioch after the persecution which arose after the martyrdom of Stephen in ca. AD 34, and from earliest records the vigour and strength of the Antiochene church can be seen. Acts 11:29 speaks of the concern of the Antiochene believers for the Judean church during a famine in the reign of Claudius, and describes how the church in Antioch collected and distributed relief for those most in need. The earliest followers of "The Way" would be likely therefore to have come from the Jewish community. In this, they would be typical of all the early Christian communities in Syria and Mesopotamia. The Christians of Antioch, however, were distinguished by speaking Syriac and thus were representative of a pure Semitic form of Christianity. Syriac is a dialect of Aramaic (the *lingua franca* of the region) prevalent in northern Mesopotamia and the adjoining eastern province, Adiabene. Syrian tradition, in the Syriac *Doctrine of Adai* speaks of Edessa (the Syriac Urhay) as the centre of West Syriac culture. This tradition tells how King Abgar of Edessa heard the gospel from the legendary Adai, one of the seventy disciples, [2] and although this Syriac document is probably no earlier than the fifth century, Eusebius (ca. 260–ca. 340) records a form of the story in connection with the apostle Thaddeus.[3] Wherever its centre lay, either in Antioch or Edessa, the Syriac-speaking church assumed great importance in the Patristic Period, and by the fourth century was prolific in its theological and liturgical output.

In this formative and dynamic period of the Syriac-speaking church of Antioch, the outstanding figure is Ignatius, who suffered martyrdom during the reign of Trajan (AD 98–117). So revered was Ignatius in Syrian tradition, that Syrian patriarchs from about the thirteenth century have taken the name Ignatius on the occasion of their consecration. Throughout this early period, very few of the patriarchs of Antioch were to live and die peacefully.[4] Martyrdom was to characterize the life of the church.

The flowering of Syriac culture and theology came, however, in the fourth century with the great theologian Ephrem the Syrian (ca. 306–376). Ephrem came from Nisibis, where he founded his theological academy before being forced by the war between the Roman and Persian Empires to move to "safety" further west at Edessa. Ephrem's work in the production of biblical exegesis and hymnography represents classical Syriac theology at its most developed. Vigorous, rich in imagery and biblical allusion, and employing the characteristically Semitic devices of parallelism and antithesis, the poetry of Ephrem has been described as the greatest of the Patristic Age, [5] and Ephrem exercised a corresponding influence on the course and future development of Syriac

Christianity. Ephrem's life was spent in Nisibis and Edessa, on the border between the Roman and Persian Empires, and it was from those two cities, in an area almost constantly affected by the warring of two hostile empires, that most of his theological output came.

This period of prolific theological output was to extend to the seventh century, and included such great figures as Jacob of Serugh (ca. 451–521) and the fourth-century Aphrahat, "the Persian sage," writing from within the Persian Empire. Syriac-speaking Christianity from its earliest beginnings has always exhibited this characteristic of existence and continued life on different sides of opposing empires.

Decline

This great period of Syriac literature was to be slowly eclipsed after the eighth century by the Arab conquest of northern Syria and Mesopotamia. The Syriac-speaking church had never accepted the Council of Chalcedon of 451, which had "resulted in the division of the apostolic Sees into two groups. The Sees of Rome and Constantinople became one group, while the Sees of Antioch and Alexandria became another."[6] There was thus not only a degree of independence from the patriarch of Constantinople and the Byzantine church, but also a degree of isolation. Like the Copts and Armenians, the Syrians place high value on their cultural and linguistic independence from the Byzantine church with its Greek thought forms and philosophy. Linguistic, cultural, and political factors thus played a major role in the split between the "Chalcedonian" and "non-Chalcedonian" churches. The Chalcedonian churches were those which accepted the theological definition of the person of Christ as being acknowledged "in Two Natures," united unconfusedly and unchangeably. The non-Chalcedonian churches (Syrians, Copts, Armenians, Ethiopians), by contrast, refused to accept the definition, and taught that the person of Christ was formed by a "Union of the Two Natures" and that therefore Christ was one incarnate nature of God the Word. The non-Chalcedonian churches thus came to be referred to as Monophysite — a term consistently rejected by the Syrian Orthodox. The early fragmentation of apostolic unity was to lead to greater linguistic and theological independence for the Syrian Orthodox, who increasingly took on the character of a "national" church. It was also to lead to a greater degree of isolation. Both of these factors together were to lead to the Syrian Orthodox welcoming the Arab conquest in the tenth century as "liberation" from the rule of the hated and despotic Byzantines, but within that welcome lay also the seeds of its decline. From its golden period of the fourth to the seventh century, the Syrian Orthodox church was to pass into a period of isolation, decline, and poverty. Only under the spiritual leadership of Jacob Baradaeus (ca. 500–578) were the fortunes of the Syriac-speaking church to revive, as he reorganized and strengthened the church in the face of Byzantine persecution. Jacob's influence was so great that Western church history often refers to the Syrian Orthodox as Jacobites, although like Monophysite, it is a term consistently rejected by the Syrians as a description of their church.

After the Arab conquest, the Syriac-speaking church was to enjoy a greater freedom of religious expression than had ever been the case under the rule of its Byzantine co-religionists. This religious peace and toleration under Arab rule was to be shattered by the advent of the Crusades, and the beginning of the fateful association in the Muslim mind of Christians with hostile governments and powers. A Coptic scholar has written, "the later Middle Ages proved to be the end of their glory and their ancient vitality. Their theological acumen and the Syriac literary genius disappeared from existence. Henceforward a poor, oppressed and shrinking minority, they lived on memories of their past heritage."[7]

The Modern Period: Contact with Anglicans
In contrast to the Apostolic and Patristic Period of the Syriac-speaking church, little is known in the West of the modern history of the Syrian Orthodox. The beginning of their contact with the Anglican church dates from the 1830s, when a general interest began to be articulated in England in the condition of the Syriac-speaking churches, both Assyrian (or East Syrian) and Syrian Orthodox (or West Syrian), within the Ottoman Empire. Contact had already been initiated with the Syrian church in South India earlier in the century, [8] but there was little continuity between the individuals and societies involved.

The earliest contact between Anglican agents and the Syrian Orthodox within the Ottoman Empire, however, took place in the 1830s and 1840s. The Royal Geographical Society sponsored an expedition to Mesopotamia in 1835 which was led by Colonel F.R. Chesney. That Euphrates Valley expedition lasted two years, and as a result, considerable interest was generated in England in the condition of the Syrian churches. In 1838, the Society for Promoting Christian Knowledge agreed to share the expenses with the Royal Geographical Society of a follow-up mission to Mesopotamia. The main concentration of the work of this expedition, led by W.F. Ainsworth and Christian Rassam, was on the Nestorians of Kurdistan, but the draft of their instructions places as much emphasis on the Jacobites as the Nestorians. This expedition was not a success; the ecclesiastical objectives were scarcely attended to, and Ainsworth returned to England with his reputation in ruins as a result of financial mismanagement. Eastern Anatolia was also in great social upheaval at the time with Kurdish rebellions dictating what was possible and what was not. For the minority Christian communities within the Ottoman Empire contact with foreign agencies, ecclesiastical or civil, was always fraught with misunderstanding and danger. Ainsworth returned to Britain in 1840, but not without first drawing attention to the presence of a missionary from the Episcopal Church of the United States of America, Horatio Southgate.

Southgate was a priest of the Episcopal church based in Istanbul from 1839, with a "brief" as "missionary to the Jacobites." Southgate was familiar with Syriac and visited the Syrian Orthodox patriarch in the patriarchal monastery of Deir-el-Zafaran at Mardin in Mesopotamia. Both Southgate and Ainsworth published the accounts of their travels and interest in the Syrian churches steadily grew within the Church of England.

In 1842, the Society for the Propagation of the Gospel (SPG) and the Society for Promoting Christian Knowledge (SPCK) mounted a joint expedition to the Syriac-speaking churches. Although the expedition's main interest was in the Nestorians, the Syrian Orthodox (or Jacobites) feature significantly in the expedition's account. The account by G.P. Badger, the expedition's leader, was published as *The Nestorians and their Rituals* in 1842, and in it Badger is less than sympathetic to the Syrian Orthodox. His views, although regarded by the Syrian Orthodox as partial and insulting, are culturally and historically conditioned. Culturally his views are conditioned by the widespread nineteenth-century British view of the British Empire as a divinely appointed instrument to civilize Eastern peoples. He wrote, "Poor people! They are in urgent need of someone to teach them the way of life." And he went on to give an interesting reason for their parlous state: "because of their monophysitism, the hand of the Lord has fallen mightily upon them." Badger then confidently predicted wherein the Syrian Orthodox salvation would lie: "I have abundant proof from the same quarter, and from the villages around, that the Jacobites here would hail with gladness, and receive with gratitude, a mission from the Anglican Church." Badger was aware of the warning that Western involvement with Eastern Christians in the Ottoman Empire could have potentially disastrous consequences for the political equilibrium in those areas where Christians lived, but chose to reject it. In 1843 and 1846, a terrible Kurdish massacre of the Nestorians happened, partly attributable to the latter's contact with foreigners, but the Syrian Orthodox were spared the full blast of the atrocities.

After Badger's mission, no official Anglican policy with regard to the Syrian Orthodox church was to emerge, and ecclesiastically the analysis of the proximity or distance of the two churches varied greatly. All the missions during this period were initiated by individuals and societies, albeit Anglican. The hierarchy of the Church of England still needed much persuasion of the wisdom and usefulness of making such contact. What communication there was was carried out in isolation from other ventures — those who were in touch with the Syrian church in the Ottoman Empire had no dealings with other individuals and societies who had contact with the Syrians in India. It was not until the late 1840s that a development was to occur which brought together the Ottoman and Indian aspects of Syrian Orthodoxy in their relations with the Church of England and Anglicans. It is therefore now appropriate to focus our concern on the Syrian Orthodox in India.

Syrian Orthodoxy in India

The existence of a Christian church in the extreme southwest coast of the Indian subcontinent, the Malabar coast, has been known from the earliest history of the church. The Christians of South India prize the tradition that their faith was introduced by St Thomas into Malabar, and called themselves the St Thomas Christians after him. Whatever the authenticity of the tradition, it is certain that the trade routes existed between the countries of the Middle East and the Malabar coast. Sea routes from Egypt through the Red Sea and from Mesopotamia through the Persian Gulf are documented in antiquity. The earliest history of Christianity on the Malabar coast is, however, obscure, but the presence of an Indian is recorded at the Council of Nicaea in 325.[9] The native Christian church appears to have had an East Syrian connection, since colonies of Jews from Mesopotamia were established on the Malabar coast for trading purposes. East Syrian literature contains references to India which is almost identical to modern India. This probable East Syrian connection of Christianity in India accounts for the fact that the Christians of South India, while using a Syriac liturgy, were labelled Nestorian. Earliest contact with the Western church was to come through Latin missionaries on their way to China in the thirteenth and fourteenth centuries and the arrival of Portuguese Catholic missionaries in the sixteenth century. However, for the Christians of South India their Nestorian label was to provoke harsh response from their newly arrived co-religionists. The Synod of Diamper in 1599 was an attempt, supported by the civil and military power of the Portuguese, to force Syrian Christians to renounce their Nestorianism and submit to papal authority. This attempt to impose an alien Latin culture and liturgy on an oriental church was to have short-lived results — in 1653, a mass revolt of Indian Syrian Christians took place, in an attempt to rid themselves of Jesuit and Portuguese influence. These Syriac-speaking Chrisitians then turned to Syriac-speaking ecclesiastical authority in the person of the Syrian Orthodox patriarch of Antioch. In 1665 the new Syrian bishop, Mar Gregorius, arrived in Malabar, and the connection between the Syrian Christians of India and the see of Antioch was formed. The position of the Syrian Orthodox patriarchate was that this connection was already in existence, even if undocumented.[10] The seeds of religious and theological dissent within the Christian community of South India had, however, been sown, and by the mid-seventeenth century, different sections of that community were to owe ecclesiastical allegiance to Rome, Antioch, and to the Nestorian patriarch.

Contact with Anglicans

This was the situation which the British were to encounter in India at the end of the seventeenth century. Chancellor Geddes produced his *History of the Church in Malabar* in 1695, and although Geddes never went to India, he relied heavily on Portuguese Roman Catholic sources, using those very sources in his work of polemic against the Roman church and hierarchy. It was not until the beginning of the nineteenth century, however, that systematic and sustained contact began to be made.

Richard Hall Kerr, a chaplain of the East India Company in Madras, had been asked by the governing body of the Fort St George settlement to undertake a study of the Syrian church in Travancore and Cochin in 1803. Kerr read his report to the authorities of Fort St George at a public consultation on 4 November 1806. The report is important for an early Anglican understanding of the Syrian tradition. Drawing on the work of the French historian, La Croze, Kerr divided Christianity in India into three groups — the St Thome or Jacobite Christians, the Syrian Catholics, and the Latins. He wrote of the Jacobite Christians' liturgy; "the service in these churches is performed very nearly after the manner of the Church of England." And in describing his interview with the metropolitan of the Syrian church, Kerr went on, "When the Metropolitan was told that it was hoped that one day a union might take place between the two churches, he seemed pleased at the suggestion."[11] Kerr clearly conceived of the Syrian church as a close sister church of the Anglican and predicted that a union was inevitable, even imminent.

Claudius Buchanan, in his *Christian Researches in Asia* (1811), also maintained the proximity of the two churches, and in 1816 an important experiment was begun in India. A seminary of the Syrian Orthodox church was set up in 1815, and the following year missionaries sent by the Church Missionary Society (CMS) began to cooperate in its work. This joint Syrian-CMS experiment was to last twenty years. Beginning with high optimism for the future of relations between the two churches, but rapidly degenerating into bitterness and rancour, the experiment was formally terminated in 1836. CMS remained an essentially protestant and evangelical society of the Church of England, and insistence on reform within the Syrian church led to the existence of an Anglican Syrian church in 1836. For this to have happened, relations must clearly have soured badly. The tension between the reforming party of those Syrians who had come under CMS influence and those Syrians who maintained a traditionalist positions was not to end with the termination of Anglican-Syrian relations in 1836. The tension continued into the 1840s and led to a dispute which was to be the cause of the coming together of Syrian concerns in the Middle East and India, already referred to.

By the 1840s, conflict was endemic within the Syrian church in India between the reformers and the conservatives. The most outstanding of those Syrians who advocated reform was Abraham Malpan. He had constructed a revised Syrian liturgy, greatly influenced by Anglican theology and practice, but was unable to carry out his reforms. In order to assure future episcopal blessing for his reforms, he arranged for his nephew to travel to the Middle East to be consecrated bishop by the patriarch. He went in 1841 and returned as Mar Athanasius in 1843. This brought him into conflict with an already established metropolitan, Mar Dionysius. Claim and counterclaim, litigation and counterlitigation were to follow between the two parties, until the bitterness and rancour engendered by the 1860s forced the two parties to seek direct patriarchal intervention. The patriarch of Antioch who was to respond to this call was the Patriarch Peter III Ignatius (1872–1896), called in Syriac tradition Peter IV. He visited England seeking, among other things, Anglican mediation in this conflict. The visit of this patriarch was to lead to the most substantial contact between the two churches in the history of Anglicans and Syrians.

India, Antioch, and Canterbury: Peter III Ignatius
The patriarchate of Peter III was to mark the beginning of a fifty-year period during which Anglican-Syrian Orthodox relations were to be more thorough and fruitful than at any period before or since. His visit was the occasion of more articulated interest

in the Syrian Orthodox church than had hitherto been the case from within the Church of England. His purpose in making the visit was two-fold according to contemporary observers. Firstly, it was to obtain material and practical support for the opening of Syriac schools in Turkey; this educational mission of help was to become an important Anglican model of cooperation for Oriental Orthodox churches. Secondly, it was to obtain from the British government official recognition of his authority over Syrian Orthodox (and British subjects) in South India, similar to the authority granted to him by the imperial firman within the Ottoman Empire. These two aims were not always distinct and were often confused, both in the mind of the man who sought the help, and in the minds of those who were approached for that help; not least, in the mind of the archbishop of Canterbury, Archibald Campbell Tait.

When Tait met the patriarch in 1874, his position was already formulated. He clearly and unequivocally supported the reforming Athanasius, and not Dionysius. His position had been formulated on the basis of information coming to him from Anglican bishops in India, in particular, the bishops of Calcutta and Madras. Tait, in his first encounter with the patriarch, went quickly to the core of the difficulty between Athanasius and Dionysius, India and Antioch — the nature of ecclesiastical power and control. In his analysis of the relationship between Malabar and Antioch, Tait asserted to the patriarch, "I venture to suggest to you for your consideration whether it is desirable to endeavour to maintain over them a control which can only be nominal over so distant a Church with which communication must be very difficult, and the members of which seem entitled to independence in the selection of their Bishops." This advice would have been unpalatable enough to the patriarch, but Tait went on to recommend a specific form of relationship between Antioch and Malabar; "there are now about one hundred and seventy Bishops of the Anglican Communion in various parts of the world, all more or less connected with the See of Canterbury, and the comparative independence which they enjoy has in no way been found to interfere with a hearty intercommunion between the several Churches over which they preside or with their attachment to the ancient See of Augustine. The Archbishop would suggest to Your Holiness whether it would not be well to adopt some similar re-adjustment of the relations at present existing between Your Holiness' See and the Christians of Malabar.'' [12]

The relationship between the two men was to fluctuate during the course of the patriarch's visit, but important connections were established at the hierarchical level between the Syrian Orthodox and Anglican churches, and important cultural contacts made.

As a result of Peter III's visit to London, the Syrian Patriarchate Educational Society was founded with the specific aim of generating funds and support for the newly opening Syriac schools in the patriarch's area. The patriarch had two audiences with Queen Victoria, and after his visit had ended, the level of knowledge of the Syrian Orthodox church within the Church of England and the wider establishment in Great Britain was infinitely higher. The patriarch was to leave Britain frustrated, however, in both his aims.

After leaving Britain, the patriarch was to go on to India to attempt a resolution of the dispute among the Syrian Christians of Malabar. When he arrived and reported the attitude of the British authorities, ecclesiastical and civil, to his appeal for support, a vociferous reaction was to result. On 11 December 1867, *The Western Mail* (published in South India) contained this analysis of the situation, a graphic description of the strength of feeling engendered by the perceived British support of Athanasius: ''If this is not tyranny and oppression calculated to make one's blood boil; and to electrify the victims into a wild and raging revolution, we do not know the meaning of tyranny and injustice . . . . Even a worm will turn if you tread on it, and it would be well not to arouse the self-preserving instincts of the down-trodden worm in the breasts of a people who have had much to suffer for the past half century.''

The dispute was sadly to drag on, and after Peter III had left India and returned to the patriarchal seat in Mardin, litigation and counterlitigation were to follow.

The Context, post Peter III

The episode of Peter III and Archbishop Tait has been dealt with in some detail because in it can be found in microcosm the entire range of Anglican attitudes towards relations with an oriental church. Often overlooked, but equally important, was the element of difficulty of communication between an oriental and an occidental church. The enterprise was fraught with difficulties of a kind which were rarely expressed directly, or of which the participants in the exchange seemed scarcely aware. After the patriarch's visit to London, relations were to grow faint yet again, and after Tait's death, the new archbishop of Canterbury, Benson, was to concentrate the Church of England's attention on Christians in the Ottoman Empire with the formal opening of the Archbishop of Canterbury's Mission to the Assyrians in 1886.

During Benson's primacy, Peter III died and was succeeded by Abdel-Mesih, whose short patriarchate was terminated in 1906 with the accession of Abdallah II. Abdallah II and his contemporary at Canterbury, Randall Davidson, were to reawaken the mutual interest in each other's churches.

Ecclesiastical exchanges do not take place in a political vacuum, and the political world of 1906 was very different from that of 1874, especially for minorities within the Ottoman Empire. The Armenian massacres had taken place, and the position of all Christian minorities within the Ottoman Empire was greatly compromised by those events in the eyes of the authorities. The Ottoman Empire was in decay and soon to collapse, and a new Turkish authority was to take its place.

Modern Turkey and Flight

The new Kemalist nation in post-Ottoman Turkey of 1922 was not sympathetic to religious minorities. The Treaty of Lausanne was, in theory, to protect the rights of religious minorities within the new Turkey, but according to domestic Turkish interpretations of that treaty, the rights of only named minorities were guaranteed — the Jews, the Greeks, and the Armenians. Since the Syrian Orthodox were nowhere named in the treaty, their existence was unofficial and their language, Syriac, illegal. This was the situation in which the Syrian Orthodox were to find themselves. The political vicissitudes which they had undergone were difficult for Anglicans to comprehend and respond to accordingly. An atmosphere of mutual distrust and caution was to characterize the political climate. An awareness of this fact was shown in the Report of the Lambeth Conference of 1920; "The present moment, when under the draft Turkish Treaty the West Syrians remain under Turkish rule, is not specially suitable for endeavouring to establish closer relations with them." After a period of almost one hundred years of contact between Syrians in the Ottoman Empire and Anglicans, that contact was to diminish.

The Syrian Orthodox patriarchate was to move from its traditional seat of Deir-el-Zafaran near Mardin in Eastern Turkey, first to Homs in Syria, and then to Damascus. The Syrian Orthodox remaining in Turkey became increasingly isolated and fearful for their existence. A report of 1926 described their condition as "depressed and dwindling." Many Syrian Orthodox had fled from Turkey into Syria during the Armenian difficulties, and with the removal of the patriarchal seat from Deir-el-Zafaran into Syria, many more Syrian Orthodox left, settling mainly in northeast Syria, the Jazira. The main waves of migration took place in 1922 and 1924, and the Syrian Orthodox rapidly began to settle in their newly found home. At the same time, they were careful to distinguish themselves from those of their co-religionists (Armenians, Greeks, and Assyrians) who had sought foreign intervention as the solution to their problems. Syrian Orthodox had also fled to Iraq, where the Arabic-speaking leadership distanced themselves from any move to look to European powers for help, at the same time pointing out that they had no intention of requesting any form of autonomy.

The far-sighted leader who emphasized this policy of support for the Arab cause was the new Syrian Orthodox patriarch, Ephrem I Barsoum. A new chapter for the history of the Syrian Orthodox in the Middle East was to open with his accession. Sophisticated, politically astute, and erudite, he was not anxious to create any ties with Christian European powers which would compromise him and his community with the new Syrian government. He was a member of the Arab academy in Damascus, and a scholar of international repute in both Arabic and Syriac. Relations with the Syrian Orthodox in the Middle East were thus to take on a different character for those from within the Church of England who had an interest in furthering relations. The Syrian Orthodox, anxious to maintain this newly found identity, were careful not to have it compromised. Even before Ephrem I Barsoum had succeeded to the patriarchate, the Syrian patriarch had written, in responding to an invitation to the Lambeth Conference of 1930, "the Syrian Orthodox are not willing to send a representative to the Lambeth Conference."[13]

A new phase had now been reached in oriental-occidental exchange. No longer could the "effortless superiority" of Western thought, culture, and theology be assumed, nor the easy association of political power with Christian faith. The new phase was to be characterized by words such as *reciprocity* and *mutual learning*. We are thus brought to the modern period.

The Modern Period

Once again, relations between Syrian Orthodox, both in India and the Middle East, and Anglicans are systematic and sustained. Under the patriarchates of Mor Jakoub III (1957-1980) and the present patriarch, Mor Ignatius Zakka I Iwas, contacts become more regular and varied. As the Anglican communion has taken increasingly the character of an international fellowship of autonomous, culturally indigenous sister churches, so the Syrian Orthodox church is now represented in more and more locations internationally. No longer is contact only in the two Syrian Orthodox heartlands, but also now increasingly in the cities of the West. Syrian Orthodox from Turkey were part of the general phenomenon of *Gastarbeiter* in West Germany during the late 1960s and 1970s — a phenomenon which almost destroyed the community in its heartland, the Tur Abdin. Indeed, emigration of Christian communities from the Middle East has been a general characteristic. Meanwhile, Syrian Orthodox from India have found themselves as *Gastarbeiter*, ironically, in the Middle East — principally, the Gulf states. A situation of social flux now exists which is constantly changing the data.

In Europe, the Syrian Orthodox church has established a diocese, monastery, and seminary, centred on Hengelo in Holland, and has begun to contribute regularly to national councils of churches throughout Europe. Syriac printing and liturgical study has undergone a revival, centred in that monastery, and a cultural focus and identity are thus sustained by the careful preservation and defence of the Syriac language.

In Turkey, after the violent days of the late 1970s and early 1980s, the small community of Syrian Orthodox in the Tur Abdin and Istanbul (approximately 42,000) is undergoing a period of relative stability and consolidation. Monastic life continues in the two principle monasteries of Mor Gabriel and Deir-el-Zafaran, and the mass exodus of the 1970s has all but stopped. The Syrian Orthodox church in Turkey is beginning to look to a future in that country.

In India, the vibrant and vigorous state of Kerala houses the largest Syrian Orthodox community. Now divided into the Catholicos party, and the Patriarchal party, the division within that church continues to reflect the disputed eccelesiastical authority and jurisdiction of the St Thomas Christians. Is the church dependent on Antioch or is it an independent church? At the time of writing, the question is not resolved, and it is not for an outsider to offer opinions on this vexed historical question. Nevertheless, it would be unfortunate if the litigation and counterlitigation between the two parties within India, in which the patriarch is not personally involved, were to continue to divert the energies of this vigorous church which has contributed so powerfully in recent times to the worldwide ecumenical movement.

But it is Syrian Orthodoxy in the Middle East which stands in most need. An indigenous Middle Eastern, Semitic form of Christianity, its existence is now in many places threatened. As an Assyrian observer has commented, "Christians of the Middle East have found themselves in the uncomfortable position of being the co-religionists of peoples and nations who were considered to be the rivals, if not the enemies, of the Muslim state. They have suffered from that position in the past and continue to feel ill at ease from it at the present."[14]

In experiencing this faith under pressure, Anglicans have much to learn of effective and appropriate solidarity with those under pressure. An experience of oriental-occidental exchange can be truly mutual, and mutually enriching. An Oriental Orthodox observer has recently written:

It is a commonly known fact that today we are facing a very decisive time in the history of the Middle East in general and of the Christian Churches therein in particular. You are well aware of the many and complex problems that we are confronting today vis a vis the resurgence of Moslem integrism, the growing pace of Western secular influence, the activities of new Christian fundamentalist groups coming from the West, the movement of emigration of Christians from this area, the social needs of the people resulting from the war situation, and the need for renewal of the local, indigenous Churches of this area, the mission of Churches *today* and other aspects of the present-day situation. All these and related issues should be seen in the concrete situation, the real context of the given facts which are quite different from those that our fathers or the generations before us faced.

The Anglican Communion is one of the Churches that has had a special link with the Middle East. I know well that the Church of England and other member Churches of the Anglican Family continue to witness in this area. It is my firm conviction that discussions, closer consultation with the Oriental Orthodox Churches are called for specifically on these matters of common ecumenical concern.[15]

Endnotes

1 Francis B. Sayre's preface to R. Brenton Bett's *Christians in the Arab East* (SPCK, 1979), p. xiii.

2 See J.B. Segal, *Edessa, The Blessed City* (Oxford, 1970), pp. 2-9.

3 Eusebius, *Ecclesiastical History*, I, 13.

4 Aziz Atiya documents the early patriarchs of Antioch in his *History of Eastern Christianity* (London, 1968), pp. 169-178.

5 R. Murray, "Ephrem Syrus," in *Catholic Dictionary of Theology*, ed. J.H. Crehan (London, 1967) II, 220-223.

6 Mar Ignatius Zakka I Iwas, *The Syrian Orthodox Church* (Aleppo, 1983), p. 24.

7 Aziz Atiya, p. 194.

8 See below, Syrian Orthodoxy in India: Contact with Anglicans

9 The best account of the different traditions of the St Thomas Christians concerning their own origins is in L.W. Brown, *The Indian Christians of St Thomas*, (C U P, 1982), pp. 43-64.

10 The present Syrian Orthodox patriarch, Ignatius Zakka I Iwas, points out that "In AD 345, a colony of Syrian Christians consisting of 72 families under the leadership of a Metropolitan and several priests and Deacons came to the West Coast of Malabar, by the direction of Mor Eustathius, the Syrian Patriarch of Antioch, and settled there. The priest who lead the revolt against the Portuguese in 1653 was from that community and this confirms the continuance of the authority of the Patriarch of Antioch until the coming of Mor Gregorius in 1665."

11 Report of Proceedings of the Fort St George Public Consultations, 4 November 1806 (India Office manuscript H59), pp. 111-112.

12 Letter of Archibald Campbell Tait to the Syrian patriarch, 23 September 1874 (Tait Papers 202, ff 237-241 in Lambeth Palace Library).

13 Letter of the Syrian Orthodox patriarch to Cosmo Gordon Lang, archbishop of Canterbury, 9 June 1930 (Lambeth Palace Library L C 153, f 129).

14 John Joseph, *Muslim Christian Relations and Inter-Christian Rivalries in the Middle East* (SUNY, 1983), p. 120.

15 Letter of the Armenian catholicos of Cilicia to the archbishop of Canterbury, Dr Robert Runcie, March 1986.

The Assyrians: The Church of the East

Henry Hill

This ancient church, known today as the Holy Apostolic Catholic Assyrian Church of the East, whose people are called East Syrians, was part of the see of Antioch until many who could not accept the Christological definitions of the Council of Ephesus (431) fled into Persia, and the church there became totally separated from Antioch. This now-separated Persian church was soon thereafter given the title *Nestorian*; (the Patriarch Nestorius of Constantinople had been condemned by the Council of Ephesus).

The Nestorian church soon initiated some of the most remarkable missionary expansions in Christian history. Driven by persecution in Persia, Christians emigrated at an early date to South India; also between the seventh and the ninth centuries they established churches far to the east in Tibet and China.

All the churches of the Middle East underwent great changes as a result of the Muslim invasions in the seventh century. In the thirteenth century the Mongol hordes brought both the West (Syrian Orthodox) and the East (Nestorian) Syrian Christian churches almost to the point of extinction. The Nestorians, once a numerous community, were reduced to mere thousands.

The community was divided in the sixteenth century by Roman Catholic missionaries who set up an alternative patriarchate among the Nestorians. Its adherents have, since that time, been called Chaldeans.

When British emissaries arrived in the 1830s the Nestorian Christians described themselves as ''Surayi''; nineteenth-century scholars in England tended to call them and their church Assyrian which mistakenly identified them with the Assyrian Empire of old. These Christians themselves called their church the Church of the East; they rarely called themselves Nestorians. The formal title today is the Holy Apostolic Catholic Assyrian Church of the

East and it has a membership of 500,000. It is not a member of the Oriental Orthodox family of churches; it accepts only the Councils of Nicaea (325) and Constantinople (381). The relationship with Anglicans is a very close one as will be seen from this chapter.

Bishop Henry Hill is the episcopal liaison between the archbishop of Canterbury, the primates of the Anglican Communion, the Oriental Orthodox churches, and the Holy Apostolic Catholic Assyrian Church of the East. Since 1980 he has been the Anglican co-chairman of the Anglican/Orthodox Joint Doctrinal Discussions. He has travelled widely among the Eastern and Oriental Orthodox churches at home and overseas, and he helped to prepare the way for this symposium which developed from the Anglican-Oriental Orthodox Forum, St Alban's, Hertfordshire in October 1985.

H.H.

The Origins

The Acts of the Apostles contains only one hint of the spread of the good news eastward. St Luke includes "Parthians, and Medes, and Elamites, and the dwellers in Mesopotamia" among the witnesses of the strange happenings on the day of Pentecost. But he makes no effort to chronicle the work of the Spirit among them. His discussion of the worldwide mission of the church deals with the movement to the west and north and south from Antioch — not to the east. Yet it was that same Antioch which was responsible for the evangelization of Mesopotamia. However, although it was only one hundred and sixty miles east from Antioch to Edessa, to make the journey was to cross a watershed — the watershed between the West and the East.

In the first century Edessa, unlike Antioch, was an independent principality separate from the Roman Empire. It stood on a tributary of the Euphrates down which trade flowed towards the Persian Gulf. The ancient caravan route to the East passed nearby. The inhabitants of the city and the surrounding district spoke a dialect akin to the Aramaic spoken by Jesus and the apostles. The city itself was likely a centre of literary culture long before the coming of Christianity; the ease and fluidity of the earliest surviving writings reflect traces of Greek influence. Clearly, Edessa was an important centre of the East, and it is not surprising that from the beginning it claimed an apostolic foundation for its church.

That claim is enshrined in the Doctrine of Adai. According to the Doctrine, King Abgar the Black of Edessa suffered from leprosy and sent a letter to Jesus asking for his help, and Jesus replied with a promise to Abgar that Edessa would be blessed.[1] After the Ascension, the Doctrine continues, Adai, one of the seventy disciples sent from Palestine, was sent to Edessa by St Thomas the Apostle to evangelize the city. When Adai came to Edessa he lodged at the house of Tobias, the son of a Palestinian Jew, who introduced Adai to Abgar. Abgar the Black was immediately healed of his leprosy and converted to Christianity with a large number of his subjects, including a community of merchant Jews. Of their history as a church we know little but this legend until the fourth century.

The political history of the region during the second and third centuries suggests a period of intermittent persecution for this church and definite isolation from the main body of the church in the West, although it remained in communion with it. Edessa itself was sacked by Roman forces early in the second century and incorporated into the new Roman province of Osrohoene around 170. The Roman imperial administration of that era was not sympathetic to Christianity.

Early in the third century Roman control in the area collapsed before the onslaught of the Persian Empire of the Sasanids; Edessa was sacked in 258. The Sasanid rulers were Zoroastrian in religion and opposed to Christianity, particularly after it became the official religion of the Roman Empire at the beginning of the fourth century. By that time, to be a Persian Christian was, in the eyes of the Sasanid King of Kings and his government, not very different from being a Persian traitor.

The official Zoroastrian religion was strongly organized throughout the Persian Empire. Priests were attached to each village and were governed by a kind of provincial bishop, the *mobed*. The chief among the mobeds (magi) was the *archimagus*, one of the most important personages in the Persian state. However, in the western provinces of the Persian Empire (such as Mesopotamia), which were largely Aramaean (Syriac) in race and language, this Zoroastrian hierarchy was little more than a facade. The religions professed by the inhabitants were as numerous as the ethnic groups which composed the mixed population.

The Christian church in that part of the Persian Empire was a melting pot. As members of a new dispensation — one in faith, hope, and love — the converts laid aside former distinctions and prejudices. An anonymous Christian's letter to Diognetus in the second century talks of one homogenous people devoted to the Lord. Bardesanes, a Syriac Christian in the Persian Empire of the third century, did not feel himself to be in any way the leader of a sect, but rather a member of the universal church. He wrote of the brethren in Gaul, Parthia, India, Persia, and Mesopotamia, without making distinction. "What shall we say about ourselves, the new race of Christians whom Christ has caused to be raised in all countries as a consequence of his coming? We are all Christians by the one Name of Christ wherever we may be found."[2] In fact, no ethnic or national distinctions could be traced because the Christians within the Persian Empire refused to write about their pre-Christian ancestors, and so we have no record of their background before the advent of Christianity.

However, the Christian community could not maintain itself as a universal people freed from the ties of politics and race. The hostility between the Roman and Persian Empires made it necessary for the Christians of Persia to build up their own ecclesiastical organization, essentially independent from that in the West. Initially, the organization of bishops, priests, deacons, dioceses, and parishes was roughly similar to that of the churches in the Roman Empire. By 313 the Sasanid persecution of the church had ended and in the *Chronicum Edessenum* chroniclers began keeping records of the bishops of Edessa and their activities.

During the first half of the fourth century a group of ascetic men and women called Sons and Daughters of the Convenant, B'nai and Bath Q'yama was incorporated into the structure of the Persian church. Aphraates, a bishop in the middle of the fourth century, after describing what was normal in the baptismal practice of his time, stated that no lay man or woman was accepted for baptism unless prepared to lead a life of strict continence and freedom from worldly cares. This meant that except for the more or less exceptional case of young devotees, the average Christian looked forward to becoming a full church member only at some advanced age, and as a prelude to retiring from the life of this world.[3]

However, by the fifth century Christianity had become the religion of most of the inhabitants around Edessa. The mass of adherents wanted to make the best of both worlds and were anxious to obtain the benefits of baptism. Parents had their children baptized in infancy and the special vows of the previous century were inappropriate. Soon there arose a Christian community in which by far the greater number of old and young were actually baptized. The old-fashioned B'nai and Bath Q'yama still continued, but it was now a sort of monastic order within the church community. Its members lived among ordinary human beings, and not as hermits in the desert or as coenobitic monks, and the church devised rules for the regulation of their course of life.

The church in Persia was represented at the Council of Nicaea in 325 by its bishop, Aitalah, and, like the church in the West, accepted the Nicene Creed. However, a local creed named after the fourth-century bishop Aphraates had acquired prominence. This Creed of Aphraates is unlike the theological expression adopted by Greek and Latin Christianity from Nicaea onward. It is first and foremost the revelation of a divine Spirit dwelling in human beings and fighting against moral evil and is not preeminently a philosophical speculation about the nature of divinity.

The Syriac (Aramaean) version of the Gospels in use in the fourth century was the Diatessaron, a gospel harmony compiled by Tatian in the first century. However, this amalgamation of the Gospels was considered to have been derived from heretical sources and was suppressed early in the fifth century. During the episcopate of Rabbula, who was bishop of Edessa between 411 and 435, the Peshitta (i.e., "simple") began to be used. It was a revision of the old Syriac version of the New Testament; thus the reading of the Four Gospels was brought into conformity with the practice in the churches in the Roman Empire.

The Churches Separate

By the first quarter of the fifth century considerable rivalry had developed between the sees of Alexandria and Constantinople and this rivarly manifested itself in a growing controversy about the definition of the divinity of Christ. The churches in the East were of course affected by the controversy and polarization that were developing, and this was particularly acute for the church in Edessa and in the Persian Empire where the situation was aggravated by the proximity of the Persian and Roman borders. Although it was by this time once again just within the borders of the Roman Empire, Edessa was becoming increasingly independent from the church in the West (including the see of Antioch) by geographical and political necessity and by reason of its disenchantment with the Roman imperial politics which lay behind the growing Christological controversy.

In 410 the Sasanid emperor summoned together eastern church leaders to the Synod of Seleucia. His purpose was to hold the catholicos of Seleucia –Ctesiphon responsible for the conduct of his people as a minority within the Persian Empire. A council of the bishops of the church in Persia was called in 424 under the leadership of the Catholicos Dadiso (421-456)[4]. The council decided that for the future religious matters should not be carried before the Western Fathers; moreover, it laid down that the catholicos in conjunction with his colleagues of the Persian kingdom was the final authority. What St Peter had been to the apostolic college, the catholicos was to be in his body of bishops. Thus the Holy Apostolic Catholic Assyrian Church of the East began its truly independent existence, and the bond, albeit a very weak one, which had attached the church in Persia to the see of Antioch (and the church in the Roman empire) was formally cut.

This cutting of the bond with the church in the West was completed doctrinally by the Council of Ephesus where the Assyrian church was not represented. The council was called in response to pressure from the see of Alexandria to determine a fuller definition of the person and nature of Christ. If the see of Alexandria seemed to stress the importance of Christ's divinity, then the sees of Antioch and Constantinople stressed the importance of his humanity. For myriad reasons the Roman see and the imperial court supported the Alexandrian position, and, as a result, the council deposed the Syrian-born patriarch of Constantinople, Nestorius, and exiled him to Upper Egypt. A number of his followers fled from West Syria to Edessa where they received support from Ibas, the head of the theological school. On this account the school was closed twice by the Roman authorities in the years 431 and 489 — the second time, finally. It was re-established at Nisibis which lay inside the Persian border. Other condemned heretics followed this flight into Persia. Alien territory had become a desired haven!

The Syrian Nestorian refugees who fled the Roman Empire were as new blood infused into the worn and harrassed body of the church in Persia. Some among the laity brought knowledge of the arts and sciences, which found them office in the land of their adoption. The clergy brought new scholarship and leadership to the church itself. Henceforth Nestorian Christianity was not to be suspect in Persia.

The significance of Nestorianism lies more in its freedom from connection with the Roman Empire than in any marked difference of faith. As Canon Prestige commented in his book *Fathers and Heretics:*

> The real theological bond between all Antiochenes was their clear perception of the full and genuine human experience which the Incarnate Son historically underwent; they shrank with horror from the idea that He was not in all respects as truly kin to us as He was to God; they emphasized the Gospel evidence of His human consciousness and moral growth, and would not have it thought that His human life was merely the illusory exhibition on earth of an action which in sphere and method was exclusively celestial.[5]

Nestorius had begun his term of office as patriarch of Constantinople in 428 by waging a sermon warfare against the use of the title *Theotokos*, or Mother of God, for the Virgin Mary, a title authorized by two hundred years of use and hallowed by popular devotion. Ordinary church people assumed that he regarded the Redeemer as an inspired man and meant to deny that he was truly God. Actually, Nestorius meant only that the Godhead preexisted before the Incarnation and was, in its own nature, unaffected by that or any other event in the temporal sphere.

From Nestorius's point of view, Cyril, the patriarch of Alexandria, was teaching a fusion of the deity and the humanity in a hybrid compound, neither wholly divine nor wholly human; whereas, what St Cyril meant was expressed in his famous statement, "One Nature and that incarnate of the Divine Word" (i.e., the concurrence of the divine and human in one person, so that whether as God or as man or as both, Christ constituted one single objective reality). Nestorius and Theodore of Mopsuestia (392-428), whom he quoted, were content to leave the union of the two natures a complete mystery; however, Cyril felt that misconceptions and heresies were bound to recur until theology had applied a positive doctrine of the one Lord Jesus Christ.

When Nestorius was eventually exiled in Upper Egypt, he seems to have lived out his life in the monastic profession which he had embraced before he was made bishop. He survived, in spite of considerable persecution, to hear an account of the Robber Council of Ephesus (449) where Cyril's extremist followers used physical violence against their opponents and so perverted Cyril's teachings that they were themselves repudiated by the Western church. Nestorius was to welcome Pope Leo the Great's Confession of Faith at Chalcedon (451): "One and the same Christ, Son, Lord, only begotten . . . made known in two natures without confusion, without change, without division, without separation."[6] It was, Nestorius asserted, exactly what he himself had always believed. He died apparently in the latter part of that same year (451). However, the political differences between East and West were so great by the time of Chalcedon that the other Oriental churches, including the West Syrian, broke from the Western church, as had the East Syrian (or Assyrian) some twenty-seven years earlier.

Actually Nestorius himself had very little prominence in this Syriac world, which seems to have attached itself more readily to the writings of Theodore of Mopsuestia. It was only later that the memory of Nestorius was restored to the church which by an accident of history has been called by his name. The present Catholicos Patriarch Mar Dinkha IV explicitly rejected the term on the occasion of his consecration in Ealing in 1976.

East Syrian (Assyrian) Missions

Meanwhile, the Assyrian church had continued to develop and expand. The school at Nisibis was becoming the greatest training ground for missionaries that Asia has ever seen. The fierce

persecutions inflicted on Christians by the Persian emperor
Shapur II (309-379) caused the emigration of considerable groups
of East Syrian refugees and missionaries to the already existing
Christian communities in Malabar in the course of the fourth
century.[7] According to tradition the relationship between the
Thomas Christians of South India and East Syrian Christianity
had found its beginning in the apostolic mission of the Apostle
Thomas.

What may be more surprising at first glance is the movement
of traders and East Syrian missionaries towards China. This was
the latter stage of that long progress eastwards with which this
chapter began. As early as the seventh century two archbishops
and more than twenty bishops in Tibet and China (east of the
Oxus River) as well as a metropolitan of China had been consecrated. This was reported in a letter from the Patriarch
Isho'yahb III, who ruled the Assyrian church from 650-660.

In 781 the progress of nearly a century and a half of missionary
expansion was celebrated by the erection of the Nestorian Tablet,
which in 1625 was unearthed at Sian-fu, the ancient capital of
Ch'ang-An. This is a slab of stone nine feet long and over three
feet wide. The front and two sides are carved with beautiful
characters, most of them Chinese but some in a strange language
which was later found to be Syriac. These were deciphered by
Chinese and Jesuit scholars who, for long afterwards, were
regarded as unbelievable frauds. We now know that the Nestorian
Tablet is the record of nearly a century and a half of Christian
history under the T'ang dynasty.[8]

The famous Nestorian Tablet is evidence of a considerable
Christian community in the heart of China. Some seventy-five
names are inscribed on it. One was a bishop and the rest were
priests or monks. After the arrival in 635 of the first pioneer north
of the Yellow River, a Syrian named Alopen, Christianity seems
to have spread throughout China. Monasteries were built in every
city, significant in number though not nearly equal to those of
the Buddhists.

The tablet reveals that the chief tenets of the "Illustrious
Religion" emphasize the Trinity and the Incarnation, but say
nothing about Christ's crucifixion and resurrection. There are indi-

cations of a considerable degree of accommodation and even assimilation of the popular religions of China in its presentation of Christianity. The expression of the faith is monastic, which undoubtedly made swift progress possible; the wooden bell for worship, the beard, the tonsure, and utter renunciation are all mentioned.

That "propitious age" ended ca 845, when the imperial favour was withdrawn; then in 907 the T'ang dynasty fell and the empire broke up into ten fragments ruled over by former provincial governors. Whether Christianity was completely stamped out of China as a result of the edict of 845 is not certain. A metropolitan of China is mentioned by the Catholicos Theodosius of Seleucia-Ctesiphon (852-868) in a list of metropolitans who could not be expected to attend the regular councils of the Assyrian church. Certainly there had always been a problem of extreme difficulty of communication between the patriarchal see of Seleucia-Ctesiphon and its daughter church in China. Perhaps the last indication of Christian activity in China was told in the words of a monk who was sent by his catholicos to China and returned to Baghdad having lost all but one of his five companions. He said that the Christians who had been of old in the lands of China were now disappeared and that their possessions had perished, so that in the whole land hardly one Christian remained alive. Though in ancient times the Christians there had possessed a church, this was also now in ruins. The monk added that when he had at length seen how there remained none of his religion, he had finally returned home, travelling back in less time than it had taken him to perform the journey out.

Whatever may have been the fate of Christianity in China, it did not completely die out in Central Asia, though at every step it had serious rivals in Zoroastrianism, Buddhism, and finally Islam. At the beginning of the eleventh century there was a remarkable mass movement towards Christianity among the Kerait Turks, who lived away to the north of Mongolia and south of Lake Baikal. We need not then be too surprised when we learn that European travellers in the thirteenth century found members of the church of the East along the road of their travels. One of these travellers was Marco Polo in 1278.

The Assyrian Church under Islam

When the Muslims first entered Persia, they do not seem to have distinguished between the different Christian sects they found there. The middle-eastern Christians helped the Arab conquerors and welcomed them as liberators from persecution from the West. ''The hearts of the Christians rejoiced over the domination of the Arabs — may God strengthen it and prosper it!'' wrote an Assyrian chronicler a few centuries after the Arab invasions. Eventually the Muslims adopted the policy of favouring the East Syrians and keeping the various Christian sects under strict control. From 987 the Assyrian catholicos was appointed by the caliph against the wishes of the other Christian communities, and three-quarters of a century later the caliph put all Christian bishops in the empire under the control of the Assyrian catholicos. He was responsible to the caliph for the Christian communities both financially and politically.

Christians were in great demand for public office in the Muslim Empire because they alone were educated. Before the ninth century not only were Christians in demand as accountants for the purposes of taxation, but also the doctors, astrologers, and philosophers were Christians. The medical school at Beth Lapat played a great part in the development of Arabic medicine. The Assyrian doctors there were teachers of the great Arabic scientists and philosophers, who in fact got their knowledge of Greek literature through Syriac translations. By the ninth century, however, the Muslims were being educated and resented Christians' holding all the best appointments.

As the Muslims were governed by their shar'ia, which included what we might call both civil and canon law, something like the millet systems of local privileges for non-Muslims was more or less inevitable. Though the disabilities under which Christians lived were irksome and humiliating, and they suffered financially, there was no persecution to the death as had been the case from time to time under the Sasanids. With the exception of the persecution by the mad caliph, al-Hakim, which lasted from 1009-1020 (when churches were destroyed and Christians were made to wear a wooden cross of five pounds weight around their necks, and a large number became Muslims) most Christian suffering was due to personal quarrels.

When the Mongols invaded the Middle East in the thirteenth century, the Christians of the area were again caught in the middle, this time between the Muslims and the Mongols. Those who found it expedient to side with the Asian invaders, hoping for more privileges, were severely punished by the Muslims. The Mongols at first favoured the native Christians over their Muslim neighbours. A number of Mongol conquerors had Christian wives, converts of Assyrian missionaries to central and eastern Asia. Conscious of the good relations between the Mongols and his Christian subjects, the caliph, al-Musta'sim, sent the Assyrian patriarch of Baghdad along with his wazir to deal with Hulagu, the grandson of the Great Khan (Genghis Khan).

Hulagu was the founder of the dynasty of the Il-khans of Persia who, though paying nominal allegiance to the Great Khan, were practically independent. Hulagu's intention was to destroy the caliphate. In 1258 he took Baghdad with terrible slaughter. The last of the Abbasid caliphs was slain. The Christians, however, were spared, for Hulagu professed himself a Christian. There is some doubt about this, but it seems his wife was a zealous member of the Assyrian church. He also had Armenian and Georgian Christians as allies. The Assyrian patriarch was given rich endowments and a former royal palace as his residence and church.

While the middle-eastern Christians welcomed the oriental invaders, the Latin Crusaders who had established kingdoms in the Middle East were alarmed by them. They feared the Mongols and actually preferred the Muslims to the native Christians whom they considered heretics who refused communion with Rome. With some hesitation the Latin barons allowed Mamluk troops to pass through Crusader territory on their way to fight the Mongols and their sectarian Christian supporters.

The absence of information about the East Syrians under later Mongol invasions should not lead us to believe that they were unmolested. Such days of continual disaster were too unsettled for the writing or preservation of history. By the time of Timur (Tamerlane) (1394), there can have been few East Syrians left, and very few Jacobites in the eastern provinces of the Muslim Empire. Many towns were devastated during the Mongol invasion, including Baghdad, Takrit, Amid, Mardin, Mosul, and Tur'Abdin. All these were formerly important Christian centres, and probably contained the greater number of Christians who had survived until then. Few can have escaped the destruction of Timur. At Amid we are told that all the inhabitants were burnt in a great fire. At Tur'Abdin, once the great centre of the Jacobites, the Christians were hunted out, and those who took refuge in underground caves were suffocated with smoke.

The Assyrian Church from the Sixteenth to the Nineteenth Century

The remainder of our tale is concerned with the later history of the East Syrians of whom less than a million are left today to bear witness to their past history.

The Catholicos Patriarch Mar Shimun, for that was always his title, was the spiritual and temporal head of the East Syrian Christians. For four hundred years, from the sixteenth century to the 1970s, the hereditary succession fell to the Abuna family; from uncle to nephew, though always chosen by popular approval and consecrated by the second-in-command, the metropolitan, or *matran*, with other bishops. The patriarchal residence was in the village of Qudshanis or Kochanis, reckoned as tribal land, where the patriarch held his court. His relations made up a sort of informal council of state and gave their advice on all matters of business. The Turco-Persian frontier was the cause of endless trouble to the Christian villagers on either side, and Mar Shimun investigated tales of wrong-doing among Turks, Kurds, and Christians, as well as in the affairs of the church.

In the nineteenth century, the East Syrian Christians made their homes in the Ottoman Empire within Kurdistan, chiefly in the mountain district of Hakkiari in the vilayet of Van. They were to be found also in the plains bordering the Sea of Urmi (Urumia), Persia, and in the hill country bordering the Turco-Persian frontier. In the Ottoman Empire these East Syrian Christians were further divided into Ashiret or tribal Syrians, who lived in the mountain fastnesses, independent of Turkish rule, paying tribute only at irregular intervals; and Rayat or subjects who lived in more open country directly ruled by Turkey. The former lived out a tribal existence comparable to that of their Kurdish neighbours, while the latter were often set upon, not only by Kurds, but by Turkish officials.

Contact with the Churches of the West

In the middle of the sixteenth century dissension developed in the East Syrian Christian community because of the confining of the patriarchate and the metropolitan's office, which consecrated the patriarch, to the Abuna family. That family was condemned by the dissenters for their consecration of and enforcement of celibacy upon unworthy minors. At the same time Roman Catholic missionaries were actively seeking conversions among the various separated churches in the East, and Jesuit priests succeeded in bringing over to Rome the Syrian Christians of India who had been closely associated with the East Syrians in Mesopotamia. In 1552 three dissenting East Syrian bishops supported Pope Julius III in his creating a Chaldean patriarchate loyal to Rome among the East Syrians. This action introduced three centuries of fierce conflict between the newly established Chaldean church in communion with Rome and the Assyrian Church of the East. Two aspects of the conflict were the enforcement of clerical celibacy among the lower clergy, and the "Romanizing" of the ancient liturgy of St Adai and St Mari.

By the seventeenth century the conflict spread among the Chaldean community and the majority, led by their clergy, severed the Roman tie, leaving only a minority in communion with the pope. A further rupture occurred in 1670, when the Chaldean patriarch, Mar Shimun XIII returned to the Assyrian Church of the East, thus restoring the patriarchal line and the continuance of that ancient family tradition which had lived on at Qudshanis. The remaining Chaldeans, loyal to Rome, created the patriarchate of Babylon which the Ottoman Empire used as a counterbalance in its dealings with the East Syrians and their church. However, the two churches suffered equally in the massacres of World War I and their relationship has been marked by increasing friendship in our own time. In December 1984 His Holiness Mar Dinkha IV and the newly consecrated bishop of California, His Grace Mar Bawai, visited Pope John Paul II in Rome in search of Christian cooperation among the two Christian communities.

Early in the second quarter of the nineteenth century the non-Roman Catholic churches of Britain and North America became aware of the Assyrian Christians who inhabited the rugged mountains of Kurdistan.

Protestant missionaries from the United States appeared in Azerbayjan (Persia) as early as 1831. The American missionaries arrived at a time of political and religious ferment when Muslim tribesmen, conquered by a superior Russian force, were in a state of perpetual rebellion and war. It was hoped that the political expansion of the Christian powers would break the power of Islam. Justin Perkins, a tutor in Amherst College, who was to live and labour in Urmiyah for thirty-six years, was told by the secretary of the American Board of Missions that his main object was to enable the Assyrian church, when renewed, to lead a Christian missionary campaign for the conversion of Islam.

In 1842 the Reverend George Percy Badger was sent from the Church of England "to make enquiries into the state and condition of the Churches of Chaldea, regarding their doctrine and discipline, the numbers of their clergy and people." He was, among other things, to seek out their needs for the Arabic scriptures and Arabic translations of the English liturgy — all of which was to be reported to the Anglican Bishop Alexander in Jerusalem and the SPG and SPCK.[9]

Badger was to become a firm friend of the East Syrians and, as a high-church Anglican, was opposed to the proselytizing programs of the Roman Catholic church in the area as well as those of the American Protestant missionaries.

Badger approached the patriarch Mar Shimun, bearing a letter dated 15 August 1842 which opened with these words:

> It is one of the pleasing signs of the times in which we are privileged to live, that a desire is felt in the different Apostolic Churches of Christ to hold out to each other the right hand of fellowship, and to endeavour by word and deed to promote each other's temporal and eternal welfare.[10]

The first point to which Badger was to direct the patriarch's attention was the assurance of the good will of the Church of England toward the Eastern Christians and "the desire which is felt in England to see their Churches restored to a flourishing condition as branches of the True Vine."[11]

However, in 1843 SPG withdrew its support; lack of funds rendered it unable to participate in anything other than colonial missions.

The jealousies and quarrels which the American missionaries had fanned by their conversions among the East Syrians burst into a conflagration only five months after the Anglican mission arrived. Under the influence of the American Protestant missionaries the Reformed Assyrian church grew and broke off from the Old Church and formed an evangelical synod — formally recognized by the Persian government.

It is impossible for us to record in detail the immediate results of Western missionary influence, other than to say that very soon afterwards the Kurdish (Muslim) army descended upon the East Syrians of Kurdistan, and the massacre that followed was the ugliest which they had experienced since the ravages of Tamerlane. This was also the first major conflict between native Christians and Muslims in modern times. About one-fifth of an East Syrian population of some fifty thousand was estimated to have been killed, when what started as a "petty feud" grew into a religious war.

Is it then possible to say anything of a positive nature about the American missionary activity of the period? The Protestant missionaries, supported by Western orientalist scholars, created modern Syriac. They built schools and engaged in a wide range of publications, not only on theological subjects but also in history, ethics, education, and literature. It was during World War I that the American missionaries proved to be the real saviours of the Christian population and thousands of Persian Kurds and Muslims as well. The name of Dr William Shedd, born in Urmiyah where his father had been a missionary before him, will ever be remembered; and the name also of Dr McDowell "who did so much for the help and comfort of our people, in the way of giving clothes, wool, etc. Always we have known him as a helper of the Assyrians, as one who has true sympathy for our people."[12]

In the face of Roman Catholic and Protestant vigour in the nineteenth century, the Assyrian Church of the East felt its isolation. Its leaders addressed a petition to the archbishop of Canterbury in 1868, requesting assistance because they had no schools of their own and "their seminaries had either been taken from them or had become the resort of the vain and the wicked."[13] As a result of this petition the archbishop of Canterbury's mission to the Assyrians was organized; it arrived in Urmiyah in 1885. Looking back in 1920 Archbishop Randall Davidson was to write:

> For more than thirty years the mission of the Archbishop of Canterbury to the Assyrian Church has had a place in the thoughts and prayers of a limited circle of friends, but it has not been largely under the public eye. During these years the remarkable series of devoted men (and women) who have been our missionaries (or, as the Assyrians call them, our Apostles), have reported constantly to Lambeth.[14]

Many have forgotten this handful of English clergy and the Sisters of Bethany who accompanied them to teach school for boys and girls in Persia — Arthur John Maclean, William Henry Browne, E.L. Curtis, W.A. Wigram, Y.M. Neesan, Athelstan Riley, and, in addition, the Committee of the Assyrian Mission.

Their school life was described by the missionaries in 1890–91 as numbering seventy-eight elementary or village schools, four high schools for boys under seventeen years, and one for girls until they married; and an upper school which was presumably a seminary for young men over seventeen, most of whom were already deacons. At the school of the Sisters of Bethany the girls worshipped at the daily morning and evening services in Mart Mariam, the oldest church in Persia. Far ahead of the missionary ideas of the time, the Anglican aim was only to aid the existing church.

Like the Roman Catholics, the Anglicans endeavoured to cultivate classical Syrian and emphasized it in their school. They discovered valuable ecclesiastical manuscripts which they published and made available to Western scholars and the Church of the East. One of these was The Liturgy of the Holy Apostles Adai and Mari with the Order of Baptism in a version still current within the Assyrian church, and also closely approximated by the Catholic Chaldeans.

The Assyrian Church in the Twentieth Century

In the tangle of events from World War I until our own time it is possible to mention only a few of the episodes in the history of the Assyrian church. It was impossible for the East Syrians to remain neutral in 1914. They placed their hopes on the Russians, who were eventually unable to save them in the face of the Muslim jihad (holy war). Led by their patriarch, the Kurdish tribes fled under very difficult circumstances to seek refuge within the Russian lines in Salmas and Urmiyah. But the Russians were obliged to withdraw from Persia as the Revolution approached in 1917, and the disappearance of their restraining influence was followed by chaos. In fact, the retreating Russian soldiers were responsible for much of the disorder that ensued, leaving a legacy of hatred and bitterness.

The British and French, recognizing the fighting qualities of the mountain tribes, made efforts to arm the Christian population; this alarmed the Muslims and led to great violence against the East Syrians.

The murder of Mar Shimun in 1917 is described by his sister. On 16 March the patriarch was invited to meet the Agha Simco, a Kurdish leader.

As Mar Shimun drove up to the house in Koni Shehr, where he was to meet with Simco, we saw that there were many men with rifles on the house roofs, but we considered that they had just gone up to see us. Simco came out to meet the Patriarch, received him with all honour, and conducted him into the hosue, where they drank tea together. Mar Shimun spoke with the utmost frankness to the Agha about peace, saying, ''I assure you in all honesty, that we have not the least intention of doing any harm in Persia, or of carving out a place for ourselves in it. We only wish to defend ourselves from the attacks of the Turks,'' and so on. Simco then replied, asserting his complete agreement with this idea, and the Patriarch rose to depart. Simco escorted him to the gate, and kissed his hand, and his horsemen were ready to conduct us on our way. Mar

Shimun and I then took our seats in the carriage, when suddenly a shot was fired at him; this was followed by a volley from the roof, from the windows, and, in fact, from all sides. As many as forty of the horsemen were killed or wounded, and in the confusion that followed some found refuge in the houses of Armenians, among whom was my brother David.

The body of the Patriarch was rescued by a party of Tiari and Tkhoma men, headed by Daniel, son of Malik Ismail. It was buried with all episcopal honours by two Bishops, Mar Petros of the Chaldean Church, and Mar Elia of our own communion. The grave is within the Armenian Cathedral of the district. Three Churches thus united to do honour to one whom all revered and loved.[15]

On 23 March the former patriarch's brother Mar Paulus Shimun XX was elected patriarch; a sickly man who was to lead his people for only two years. The arrival of the British in the area brought further hardship. The whole population, with their cattle and belongings, poured southward in appalling confusion to join the British, with the Turks and Kurds on their heels. The story of how thousands of these refugees and Kurds and Turks suffered and died through famine is the ugly story of war.

The Assyrians were eventually transported to Iraq by the British, their longing for their "old homegrounds" unfulfilled. They were in exile. In September 1919 the patriarch's able sister Surma d'Bait Mar Shimun, went to England where the question of attending the Paris Peace Conference was considered, but not acted upon. She pleaded,

What we feel now is this. We Assyrians fought for England in the war, we were recognized as her ally, if a small one; we have been sheltered by her, and are sheltered now. We do not wish you to feel that we are ungrateful for that. Yet, when those for whom we have fought have won the war, we find ourselves still exiles; still we are kept out of our country, and even the fact that our young men are fighting for England at this hour does not give us back our homes and ruined Churches.

Our people do not and cannot know how hard it is to settle things after the war; they only see that those who fought against England are in their homes, while those who fought for her are in the wilderness still. Is it so strange that they should ask, "Why is this?"[16]

Nevertheless, it was preferable to be in Iraq under British mandate than in Mesopotamia. Special recommendations were suggested for local autonomy in their new homelands or in the vilayet of Mosul in Iraq, but the situation was an impossible one. The kingdom of Iraq was too fragile to support autonomous Christian minorities within its confines, especially since the League mandate was to expire in 1935. The Assyrians become increasingly divided among themselves as it grew clear that their future would have to be assimilation within the frontiers of Iraq.

After the Iraqis assumed control of the mandate territory in 1935, the patriarch, Mar Eshai Shimun XXIII, a young man of 23, was informed by the minister of the interior that the government could not agree to transfer temporal power to him and that his position would be the same as that of other spiritual leaders. His reply was often repeated; he desired to see his people settled as loyal Iraqi citizens, but the possession of his temporal authority had descended to him from centuries past, "as a legalized delegation of the people — and it is only for them to take it away."[17]

By 1938 Mar Shimun and many of his community, including his aunt, Lady Surma d'Bait, had become refugees in the USA. Some members emigrated to Syria because it was under French mandate, while others moved to Europe and Australia and Canada. Some remained in their pre-war homes, holding their villages, like their neighbours, by prescriptive right. Mar Shimun always acted as an emissary at meetings of the leaders of his dispersed people. He was sent to defend the Assyrian cause, without success, before the League of Nations. In the U.S.A. Mar Shimun lost popularity on account of his marriage, which was a breach of almost sacred tradition, although not of the canons of the church. In 1975 he was tragically assassinated in Los Angeles. The election of the new patriarch, an historically momentous event, is described below:

There was no member of the Patriarchal family to succeed him and for the first time in centuries an election to the Patriarchate had to take place. The custom of hereditary succession had come to an end.

Thus it was that in the summer of 1976 the then Bishop of Teheran, Mar Dinkha, made a study visit to the U.K. This visit enabled Anglicans in this country to hear at first hand how developments towards the election of a new Patriarch were progressing. Bishop Mar Dinkha stayed in London, at Mirfield and at Salisbury and Wells Theological College, and was assured by friends of the Assyrian Church that the Church of England would continue to do all it could to support his Church.

The Bishop was also Chairman of the Episcopal Standing Committee of his Church and during his stay in England it became clear, after soundings in the Middle East and the Diaspora, that it might be possible to hold a Council of the Church in that country in the near future; neutral soil politically and ecclesiastically. First of all the Episcopal Standing Committee met in London, with representatives from the Middle East and the U.S.A. and the decision was taken to hold the Council during the autumn at the Anglican Benedictine Priory of St. Paul at Alton.

The Council of the Church of the East duly took place at St. Paul's Priory from the 12th to the 26th October. It unanimously elected Bishop Mar Dinkha to the Patriarchate, and further raised Bishop Mar Narsai of Lebanon to the status of Metropolitan and Assistant Patriarch.

On Sunday 17th October their 'consecration' was celebrated at St. Barnabas Ealing, for many years the spiritual home of the London Assyrian congregation. Mar Dinkha was consecrated in the context of the Holy Q'rbana (Communion) by Mar Timotheous, Metropolitan of India; Mar Narsai, Bishop of the Lebanon; Mar Youkhanan Abraham, Bishop of Syria, and Mar Aprim Khamis, Bishop of the U.S.A. and Canada. Other Assyrian Churches were represented at the service. Bishop Leonard Ashton of Cyprus and the Gulf represented the Archbishop of Canterbury, and Bishop John Satterthwaite of Fulham and Gibraltar was also present in the Choir.[18]

Under the leadership of its catholicos patriarch, the Holy Apostolic Catholic Assyrian Church of the East has become actively involved in the ecumenical scene. There are intimate links with Lambeth and the Vatican. One of its bishops is a member of the central committee of the World Council of Churches. Here in Canada it has become customary for the Anglican bishops to welcome the Assyrian bishop, when available, to the fellowship of their meetings.

It has been said often in East Syrian (Assyrian) circles that of all the churches in Christendom, it is only the Anglican which has not tried to do them any harm. We are grateful for this! But how much are we serving one another in the cause of Christ?

Appendix

Worship and Customs

The Liturgy of Mar Adai and Mar Mari is a most precious possession of the Assyrian church, different in form from the liturgies of the Antiochene school. The ancient liturgy of the church of Edessa is said to be buried within it. From a reading of the foregoing, one can only imagine the destruction of church and other documents occasioned by the persecutions and migrations of this ancient people.

It may be useful to include a few comments about religious customs as seen through the eyes of a friendly observer.

As it stood in the nineteenth century, the patriarchal church of Mar Shalita in Qudshanis may be said to be typical of most in the East in form and arrangement; its exceptions are that it is perched upon and built into the side of a rock, and the body of the church is of hewn stone. Between the sanctuary and nave stands a solid screen with only a single door covered by a curtain, drawn except at certain points of the service. To the east of the screen and on the right is a small room which serves as both baptistry and sacristy; the sanctuary is a larger room on the left and contains the altar under a stone canopy. On the altar are the cross and two candlesticks and the book of the Gospels; and in recesses in the sanctuary walls are the chalice and the paten and the holy oil. Three steps below the sanctuary arch stands a quasi-altar on which is placed the cross and a Gospel book; the altar is called the *shkhinta* (a feminine form of *schechinah*).[19] The cross is kissed by the worshippers as they enter church; the Assyrians use no crucifix or pictures. In Qudshanis there were two other tables, one to hold the service books and the other for the censer and a lamp. Another room on the south wall was used for baking the holy loaves for the eucharist.

The Assyrians emphasize the continuity of the eucharist by the unity of the bread used. Each time it is baked, it is leavened with some dough from the last baking, and thus a small portion of the holy leaven is handed on from age to age in each church. There is a legend connected with the leaven, which is believed to have been handed down from the founders of the church, Mar Adai and Mar Mari, the two apostles sent from Jerusalem after Pentecost. This leaven is renewed from time to time on Maundy Thursday with a special office by a priest and deacon. What remains in the vessels is mixed with dough, salt, and olive oil, and leavens the whole; no eucharist can be celebrated without it.[20]

The general structure of the church building in the Western world seems not unlike our own. The altar is simple, with a plain cross and two candles; a curtain is drawn in front of the sanctuary at the solemn times of the Mass; and the clergy remove their shoes when they enter the holy place. The eucharist must always be celebrated by a priest and a deacon. The language is ancient Syriac and one often hears the priest addressed as "rabbi."

There are no pictures in the church; it is doubtful if they were ever used. No doubt the influence of Islam would have brought about their disuse, even if they had ever been introduced. Their place is taken by the cross, to which the faithful pay the greatest veneration. They kiss the cross on entering the church and they never tire of signing themselves and everything that is to be consecrated, with it. They put their fingers to their mouth and say: "In the name" and then to their forehead and say, "of the Father", then to their breast at "and of the Son", the right shoulder at "and of the Holy", and to the left shoulder at "Ghost"; thus they reverse the Western way of blessing.

The Assyrians, like the Oriental Orthodox, pray standing. The tradition of kneeling is almost lost, though the clergy and faithful frequently prostrate themselves during the service, making reverent ejaculations. Prayer is always to the east; for our Lord will, they say, appear there at his second coming.

A hymn most frequently used, is the *Gloria in Excelsis Deo*, which we think of as an exclusively Latin hymn; but it is actually as universal as the church. To the hymn of the angels (Lk 2.14), additions were made, until by the fourth century, the Greek version known as the *Morning Hymn* had evolved.

But, like the church itself, it enjoyed an eastern progress which is more astounding. It was sung in a slightly different and length-ened form, by the Assyrian Church of the East; and this version, still in use among them, was in the eighth century translated into Chinese in an even longer version, called *The Hymn of the Saved to the Trinity.*

It is sung each day at the morning service, in their ancient ton-gue. Indeed, it is attached to the phrases of the Lord's Prayer at the beginning of the eucharistic liturgy and at other times as well.

First the priest begins. ''In the name of the Father and of the Son and of the Holy Spirit for ever. Glory to God in the highest'' (repeat three times) ''and on earth peace and good hope to men, at every season and for ever; amen. Our Father Which art in heaven hallowed be Thy name. Thy kingdom come. Holy, holy, holy art Thou. Our Father Which art in Heaven. Heaven and earth are full of the greatness of Thy glory. Angels and men cry to Thee, Holy, Holy, Holy art Thou. Our Father Which art in heaven hallowed be Thy name. Thy kingdom come. Thy will be done, as in heaven so on earth. Give us the bread of our need to-day. And forgive us our debts, as we also have forgiven our debtors. And lead us not into temptation, but deliver us from the evil. For Thine is the king-dom and the power and the glory for ever and ever amen. Glory be to the Father and to the Son and to the Holy Spirit, from everlasting and for ever and ever amen. Our Father Which art in heaven hallowed be Thy name. Thy kingdom come. Holy, Holy, Holy art Thou. Our Father Which art in heaven. Heaven and earth are full of the greatness of Thy glory. Angels and men cry to Thee, Holy, Holy, Holy art Thou.''

> (From The Order of the Hal-lowing of the Apostles. Made by Mar Adai and Mar Mari, the Blessed Apostles.)

A useful publication concerning worship and customs is: *The Voice from the East,* a quarterly magazine of the Assyrian Church of the East.

U.S.A. — P.O. Box 25264, Chicago, Ill.
Canada — P.O. Box 1448, Station B, Weston, Ont. M9L 2W9
U.K. — 89 Leighton Rd., Ealing, London W13
Australia — P.O. Box 621, Fairfield, Aust. NSW 2165

The Liturgy of the Holy Apostles Adai and Mari

There are three anaphoras: first, that of the apostles Adai and Mari, for Sundays — which are unique in that they address the second person of the Holy Trinity.

After the Sanctus the priest continues:

> With these heavenly hosts we confess Thee, O my Lord, (repeat), even we thy servants, weak, frail and miserable. For Thou hast shown great mercy unto us, which cannot be repaid in that Thou didst put on our humanity that Thou mightest quicken us by Thy divinity, and Thou hast exalted our low estate and hast restored us from our fall, Thou hast raised us out of a state of death and Thou hast forgiven our debts and justified us from our guilt. Thou hast enlightened our knowledge, and hast condemned, O our Lord and our God, our enemies, and hast granted victory to the weakness of our frail nature in the abundant mercies of Thy grace.

At this point, the words of institution are recited, though they were not written in the apostles' liturgy. The publishers note: "It is thought they were always recited and it is in this part of the service that they are found in the other East Syrian Liturgies."

The other eucharistic prayers are those of St Theodore of Mopsuestia (called the second prayer by the Chaldeans) and St Nestorius (the third prayer of the Chaldeans).[21]

The faithful receive the eucharistic bread in their hands in much the same manner as Anglicans; and they also receive the chalice, which Chaldean Catholics do not. This writer has administered the sacrament at the Holy Liturgy on several occasions.

The Creed of Aphraates

For this is Faith:

When a man shall believe in God, the Lord of all,
That made the heavens and the earth and the seas and all that
  in them is,
Who made Adam in His image,
Who gave the Law to Moses,
Who sent His Spirit in the Prophets,
Who sent His Messiah into the world;
And that a man should believe in the bringing to life of the dead,
And believe also in the mystery of Baptism:
This is the Faith of the Church of God.
And that a man should separate himself
from observing hours and sabbaths and months and seasons,
and enchantments and divinations and astrology and magic,
and from fornication and from revelling and from
vain doctrines, the weapons of the Evil One, and
from the blandishments of honeyed words, and
from blasphemy and from adultery,
And that no man should bear false witness,
and that none should speak with double tongues:
These are the works of the Faith that is laid on
the true Rock which is the Messiah, upon whom all the building
  doth rise.

An Excerpt from the Nestorian Tablet

35 Whereupon [one Person of] our Trinity became incarnate.
The Illustrious, Honoured-One, Messiah,
hid away his true majesty,
and came into the world as a man [or among men].
An angel proclaimed the joy.
40 A virgin bore a Sage in Syria [Ta Ch'in].
A bright star was the propitious portent.
Persians saw its glory and came to offer gifts.
He fulfilled the Old Law of the Twenty-Four Sages'
discourses, [i.e., the Old Testament, a name in

accordance with Rabbinical tradition.]
governing tribes and nation according to great
principles.
45 He established the New Religion of the Triune
Holy Spirit's silence,
refashioning good works according to right faith.
He determined the salvation of the Eight Stages,
[The Beatitudes]
refining the earthly and perfecting the heavenly.
He revealed the gate of the Three Constants,
[Perhaps the Three Great Commandments of Mt 23.
37-40 and Mt 7:12, as quoted together in the Didache 1:2]
unfolding life and destroying death.
51 He hung a brilliant sun which scattered the regions
of darkness.
The Devil's guile, lo, he has utterly cut off.
He rowed Mercy's Barge which took him up to the
courts of light.
The souls of men, lo, he has already saved.
55 His mighty task once done, at noonday he
ascended into Heaven.
The Scriptures, left in twenty-seven books,
take up the work of creation and open the spiritual
realm.
Holy baptism of water and the Spirit
cleanses from vanity and makes clean, innocent
and white.
60 We hold as our seal the cross,
which blends the four shinings, uniting all without
distinction.
We strike the wood, a voice which quickens loving-kindness.
Worshipping towards the east, we hasten on the
road to life and glory.
We retain the beard to show that we have outward
virtue.
65 We shave the crown to show that we have no inner
lusts.
We do not keep slaves, but in the outside world level
the distinction, between noble and commoner.

We do not amass possessions, but among ourselves
declare utter renunciation.
We fast in secret, and our senses have a guiding
principle.
We abstain in quietness, and our watchfulness
makes us stable.
70 Seven times a day we worship and praise,
a great protection for the living and the dead.
72 Each seventh day we sacrifice
to cleanse the heart and regain our purity.
The True and Eternal Way [Tao] is wondrous and
hard to name.
75 Its active energy is clearly manifest.
Hence it may be called "The Illustrious
Religion".
If there is only a Way [Tao] and no Sage, it will
not expand.
If there is a Sage and no Way, nothing great will
result.
When a Way and a Sage are found together,
80 Then the Whole Empire is cultured and enlightened.
At the time of T'ai Tsung, cultured Emperor,
whose shining glory opened a propitious age,
who was an enlightened Sage over his people,
in Syria (Ta Ch'in) there was a Bishop (Lofty
Virtue) named Alopen."[22]

Endnotes

1 Eusebius, *Ecclesiastical History* (New York: Fathers of the Church, Inc.,
   1955), 1:13. Jesus' letter, with the exception of the clause of blessing, was recorded by Eusebius. He probably excluded the blessing
   because he knew of the subsequent sack of Edessa by Lucius Quintus
   under the Emperor Trajan (AD 115-116) and the absorption of the
   province of Osrohoene into the Roman Empire in AD 170.
2 ibid., 1:4.
3 F.C. Burkitt, *Early Eastern Christianity* (London: John Murray, 1904),
   p. 129.

4   Louis Duchesne, *The Early History of the Christian Church from its Foun-dation to the End of the Fifth Century* (London: John Murray, 1910-1924), 3:389. Catholicos is generally the title given to the leading bishop of a church outside the Roman Empire.

5   G.L. Prestige, *Fathers and Heretics* (London: SPCK, 1948), p. 133.

6   J.N.D. Kelly, *Early Christian Doctrines* (New York: Harper and Brothers, 1960), pp. 339-340.

7   The account of how the Syrian church of St Thomas emerged on the scene of history with close ties and contacts with the see of Seleucia-Ctesiphon by the mid-fifth century is told in William H. Tay-lor's essay in this book.

8   John Foster, *The Church of the T'ang Dynasty* (London: SPCK, 1939), pp. 136-138.

9   G.P. Badger, *The Nestorians and Their Rituals* (London: Masters, 1853), 1:xv.

10   ibid., 1:xiv-xviii.

11   ibid., 1:xiv-xviii.

12   Surma d'Bait Mar Shimun, *Assyrian Church Customs and the Murder of Mar Shimun* (London: Faith Press, 1920), p. 107.

13   ibid.

14   ibid., p. vii.

15   ibid.

16   ibid., pp. 113-114.

17   ibid.

18   Christopher Hill, ''The Nestorians and Their Patriarch'' (an unpub-lished paper).

19   *Shechina* is a Hebrew word for the overwhelming power of God over the tabernacle which led the people of Israel through the wilderness.

20   The writer remembers an Assyrian priest and deacon baking loaves in the kitchen oven of the Anglican sisterhood of St John the Divine in Toronto, with proper prayers and ceremonies, and hearing one of the sisters say that never before to her knowledge had incense been used in the convent kitchen. The eucharist, the Holy Qurbana, was celebrated the next morning; Anglicans and members of the Church of the East communicated together.

21   *The Liturgy of the Holy Apostles Adai and Mari* (Urmi: Press of the Arch-bishop of Canterbury's Mission, 1890).

22   Foster, pp. 136-138.

Bibliography

Atiya, Aziz S. *A History of Eastern Christianity*. London: Methuen, 1968.

Badger, George P. *The Nestorians and Their Rituals*. 2 vols. London: J. Masters, 1853.

Browne, Lawrence E. *The Eclipse of Christianity in Asia from the Time of Muhammed till the Fourteenth Century*. Cambridge: Cambridge University Press, 1933.

Burkitt, F. Crawford. *Early Eastern Christianity*. St Margaret's Lectures on the Syriac Speaking Church. London: John Murray, 1904.

"Chaldean Rite." *New Catholic Encyclopedia*. New York: McGraw Hill, 1967.

Duchesne, Louis, *The Early History of the Christian Church from its Foundation to the End of the Fifth Century*. Vol. 3. London: John Murray, 1910-1924.

Eusebius Pamphili, *Ecclesiastical History*. 2 vols. New York: Fathers of the Church, Inc., 1955.

Foster, John. *The Church of the T'ang Dynasty*. London: SPCK, 1939.

Hill, Christopher. "The Nestorians and Their Patriarch." Unpublished work.

Hitti, Philip K. *Syria, A Short History*. New York: Macmillan, 1959.

Jalland, Trevor. *Life and Times of St Leo the Great*. London: SPCK, 1941.

Joseph, John L. *The Nestorians and Their Muslim Neighbours*. Princeton: Princeton University Press, 1961.

————. *Muslim-Christian Relations and Inter-Christian Rivalries in the Middle East*. Albany: State University of New York Press, 1983.

Kelly, J.N.D., *Early Christian Doctrines*. New York: Harper and Brothers, 1960.

Latourette, Kenneth Scott. *A History of Christianity*. London: Eyre and Spottiswoode, 1954.

The Liturgy of the Holy Apostles Adai and Mari. Urmi: Press of the Archbishop of Canterbury's Mission, 1890.

Maclean, Arthur J. and William H. Browne. *The Catholicos of the East and His People*. London: SPCK, 1892.

Piepkorn, Arthur C. *Profiles in Belief: The Religious Bodies of North America*. Vol. 1. New York: Harper & Row, 1977.

Prestige, G.L. *Fathers and Heretics*. Bampton Lectures. London: SPCK, 1948.

Surma d'Bait Mar Shimun. *Assyrian Church Customs and the Murder of Mar Shimun*. London: Faith Press, 1920.

The author is sincerely indebted to Dr Esho Marcus, the official historian of the Church of the East, for much material in this chapter.

The Oriental Orthodox Churches and the Assyrian Church of the East and Early Lambeth Conferences

Christopher Hill

This chapter is culled from the records of the Lambeth Conferences between 1867 and 1920 kept at Lambeth Palace, and studied by very few if any scholars until the present time. The evidence shows a sustained interest in Anglican relationships with the Oriental Orthodox and the Assyrian churches of the east which was essential for the renewed understandings between our communities.

Christopher Hill has found time to supply this valuable information for us in time snatched from his many and very demanding duties as the archbishop of Canterbury's secretary for ecumenical affairs. His office is a continuation of the former Council on Foreign Relations which pioneered Anglican contacts with overseas churches after the Lambeth Appeal of 1920. These included many contacts with the Oriental Orthodox churches and the Assyrian Church of the East in the United Kingdom and in their homelands.

H.H.

Comtemporary Anglican relations with the Oriental Orthodox churches are characterized by the word "pastoral." This was how the Anglican-Oriental Forum was described in 1985. Behind the word lies a certain *de facto* recognition of each other as churches set in particular cultures; churches which have never claimed to be more than part of the One, Holy, Catholic, and Apostolic Church; churches which place a high value on their continuity with the apostolic past. Behind the use of the word also lies a sense of the pastoral assistance the churches need to give to each other, especially the support which Anglicans should feel obliged to give to Christian brothers and sisters in places where Christian witness is not easy — and has not been easy for centuries.

It is important for Anglicans to remember that the "pastoral" agenda has never been absent from our dealings with the Oriental Orthodox, as will become apparent in this summary of five early Lambeth Conferences (1878-1920). This is not to say that theological issues were not present — especially in 1908 and 1920 — but the theological issues were set within the broader context of Christian traditions which recognized the true Church of Christ in each other and also saw the mutual pastoral obligation this recognition imposed.

1867

Although the first Lambeth Conference of 1867 had the reunion of Christendom at the top of its agenda, it was not a conference which in fact materially altered Anglican attitudes to other churches. Its real agenda was the nature of the Anglican communion and the resolving of internal tensions. There was no mention of the Oriental Orthodox in its reports or resolutions, nor were they discussed in its committees or correspondence.

1878

In the preparation of the 1878 Lambeth Conference the Oriental churches already begin to appear on Anglican agendas. The bishops of the communion were invited to write to the archbishop of Canterbury, Campbell Tait, informing him of subjects which required discussion. In a letter to the archbishop, Charles Sandford, bishop of Gibraltar, stressed the need to help "our Oriental brethen" — in which he included both the Eastern Orthodox and Oriental Orthodox churches which he saw in need of education and some reformation. Bishop Alexander Greg of Texas asked for the relation between the Armenian and Anglican churches to be investigated "that there may be no conflict between the two" where territories overlapped. Gregory Bedell of Ohio requested the conference to look at the Oriental churches so that it could decide "which of them are to be deemed as Orthodox." The Association for the Promotion of the Unity of Christendom presented a "memorial" to the bishops which included a plea for the Armenians. This early correspondence therefore already contains the range of issues which was to be developed more fully in later conferences and is still with us today: theological education; the Oriental diaspora jurisdictions; strictly dogmatic issues between Anglicans and Oriental Christians; and political support for churches in difficult circumstances.

At the conference itself Archbishop Tait gave a remarkable testimony to the sense of fellowship which was developing between the Anglicans and the Oriental Orthodox. The archbishop of Canterbury was the chairman of the committee dealing with miscellaneous matters raised by the bishops. In fact, in reporting to the conference on behalf of his committee he raised relations with the Oriental Orthodox as something he was particularly concerned with himself at Lambeth. The minutes are worthy of extensive quotation.

Tait introduced the question of relations with churches "which are not integrally, or in any distinct way united in communion with the Anglican Church" and had appealed for help. After speaking of the Old Catholics he immediately catalogued the "Armenian, Syrian, Chaldean and Nestorian" churches as having brought "their cases of late years either through myself or in some other way before the authorities of the Church of England." He went on, "There can be no doubt that there is at the present moment in the East a strong desire manifested to enter into some sort of distinct relation with the Church of England."

The archbishop illustrated this by describing at some length one particular appeal, that of the Assyrian church. At the request of the Assyrian patriarch, an Anglican priest, Mr Cutts, was sent to visit the Assyrian community "in the mountains which lie between Persia and Armenia." The archbishop then told the conference of the findings of this visit, "of the way in which he was received by the Patriarch, and of the enormous gathering from all the various small communities within reach of the Patriarch's dwelling, so that more than a thousand persons assembled to welcome him as the representative of the Church of England."

Tait then explained some Anglican "difficulties," particularly the lack of education in the Assyrian church and the hereditary Assyrian patriarchal succession. These he saw as "very alien to our own habits and modes of thinking in this country." But he had "every reason to suppose that (the patriarch) was perfectly sincere in his desire to enter into these relations, and the throng which gathered round Mr Cutts seemed to imply that there was a strong feeling, on the part of these Christians everywhere, to rally round this connection with the Church of England."

The archbishop, however, noted another difficulty. Was his emissary looked upon as a representative of the state as well as the church? "In those parts of the world it is very difficult to separate the idea of a civil officer and an ecclesiastical officer. Every Patriarch in the Turkish dominions is, as I understand, a Civil officer over his own people. He is their judge and exercises various rights of the civil magistracy, subject to the Sultan." Tait saw the possibility of real confusion between an English clergyman and a British consul, especially since French consuls had represented Roman Catholicism and Russian officers the Eastern Orthodox church.

Tait then delicately asked whether the Oriental churches were really disposed to enter ecclesiastical relations with the Church of England so

> as to remove from their services — not perhaps their ancient services, but the services which have grown up in the course of ages of degradation and ignorance — things which are not congenial to the doctrine and discipline and thoughts of the English people; or whether they are rather seeking such a recognition on the part of the great English nation represented by its Church, as would save them, in the civil contests to which they have been exposed for many years, — save them perhaps from pillage and extortion, and from all ill-treatment, to which they have been very liable to be subjected in past times.

Tait recognized another difficulty of quite a different kind: the American Protestant missionary who in evangelizing and proselytizing had instigated reform movements within the Oriental churches — particularly the desire for free access to the Scriptures. But Tait also went on to recognize

> that there is this feeling also among the people, that they do venerate the old constitutional system, which has come down

in the outward Church government from the days of the Apostles: and that an obstacle is presented in the way of their receiving purer views of Gospel truth from the fact that it is presented to them by persons who have entirely abandoned the old traditions to which they have become accustomed.

Tait repeated that the Assyrian example he had been speaking of extensively seemed ''as a sort of sample'' of the issues contact with the Oriental churches raised for Anglicans. Tait went on to speak of appeals to him by the Syrian church in Malabar in its dispute with the patriarch ''from Mesopotamia'' and of an appeal from the Chaldean church in India ''claiming to be united, not with this Patriarch from Nineveh, but with the Patriarch of Babylon.'' Finally Tait told the Lambeth fathers of a personal appeal from the Armenians in the shape of ''the ex-patriarch of the Armenians . . . who did me the honour to wait upon me on his way to the great Conference of the Civil Powers at Berlin.''
The archbishop concluded:

But all this shows that the whole world is seeing that persons, connected with these ancient Churches at the present moment, are anxious to look to the Church of England. Therefore, in my opinion, the Church of England is under a most serious responsibility, not to turn a deaf ear to any request which is made to it from any of these ancient Churches.

Ironically, Tait then lamented that an appeal brought back by Mr Cutts for two Anglican priests to go out to instruct Assyrian seminarians had so far produced no results. He appealed to the Lambeth fathers for help of a ''distinctly practical kind'' to give ''a more practical turn to this union between ourselves and the ancient Churches.''
Archbishop Tait's desire to give practical help to the Assyrians took effect only with his successor Archbishop Edward Benson. He refounded the Archbishop of Canterbury's Mission to the Assyrians in 1885, after which educational work among the Assyrians was put onto a more systematic footing, builing on the early work of the Reverend Joseph Wolff of the British and Foreign Bible Society, and especially the pioneering liturgical achieve-

ments of the Reverend George Percy Badger between 1842-44. The Archbishop's Mission continued until the outbreak of the First World War.

1888

A Syrian Orthodox bishop, Mar Gregorius of Homs, was present in Canterbury at the beginning of the Lambeth Conference of 1888. Bishop Perry of Iowa described his colourful presence, representing the patriarch of Antioch, as " conspicuous in his quaint head-gear and long, flowing robes." Mar Gregorius was in England principally to seek aid from the Church of England in the re-establishment of the Syriac printing press (which had been projected as far back as the visit of Patriarch Peter III to London in 1874-5) and the establishment of the Syrian Patriarchate Education Society.

By the 1888 Lambeth Conference general relations between the Anglican communion and the Eastern churches warranted a special item on the agenda. Two major speeches were made by bishops with direct experience of the Eastern churches.

The bishop of Gibraltar spoke to the conference of the great friendliness of the Orthodox. But he was also realistic in recognizing that the Eastern churches looked to Anglicans with more than one motive. Anglicans were seen as a defence "against Turkish misrule and Roman aggression." The Anglican policy of not proselytizing was deeply appreciated. The bishop spoke of the Eastern churches as "sister-churches" and looked for intercommunion "in God's own time."

The next speech came from the bishop in Jerusalem. After a positive beginning he cautioned against overhaste by unauthorized amateurs, adding that, "Such rashness has for the moment almost closed our intercourse with the Coptic Church." He cited difficulties of practice as well as dogma, notably infant confirmation or chrismation which he argued Anglicans should recognize as valid. The archbishop of Canterbury proposed the establishment of a conference committe to draw up a report on relations with the Eastern churches. This was unanimously accepted.

The bishop of Winchester, Dr Harold Browne, became chairman of the committee, which, after dealing with relations with the (Greek) Orthodox, went on to speak of the Oriental churches. The committee first spoke of the Armenian church, which it regarded as numerically most significant — this was, of course, before 1917:

> Approaches have been made to us from time to time by Bishops and other representatives of this communion, appealing for aid in support of educational projects.

The committee then delicately touched on dogmatic issues:

> The Armenian Church lies under the imputation of heresy. But it has always protested against this imputation, affirming the charge to have arisen from a misconception of its formularies. The departure from orthodoxy may, perhaps, have been more apparent than real; and the erroneous element in its creed appears now to be gradually losing hold upon the moral and religious consciousness of the Armenian people.

The committee then spoke of "our position in the East as involving some obligations to the Oriental Church." This was presumably a reference to the influence of Anglicans in the Middle East due to an expanding empire and British sphere of influence, though two of the members of the seven member committee were bishops of the Episcopal church in the U.S.A. The committee noted a certain diminishment in the moral spiritual life of the Coptic, Ethiopian, Syrian, and Assyrian communities but went on to:

> recollect that but for them the light of Christianity in these countries would have been utterly extinguished, and that they have suffered for many centuries from oppression and persecution.

So Anglicans were encouraged to help the Oriental churches to improve their conditions and to seek "the unity of the faith without prejudice to their liberty." The committee instanced the Archbishop of Canterbury's Mission to the Assyrians as an example of such assistance. Curiously there is no mention of the

Syrian Patriarchate Education Society or the Syriac printing press Mar Gregorius had requested.

The encyclical letter and resolutions (in their final form) did not draw distinctions between the Orthodox churches in communion with Constantinople and the Oriental Orthodox churches. But the encyclical spoke of the Eastern churches as having "well earned the sympathy of Christendom, for through long ages of persecution they have kept alive in many a dark place the light of the Gospel."

The conference went on to urge brotherly charity, indulged in some criticism of Roman Catholic policy in the Middle East, and claimed that proselytism was an improper approach to these ancient churches.

Resolution 17 endorsed this approach and expressed the hope that "barriers to fuller communion" might be overcome. Internal reformation, rather than conversions, was encouraged. In presenting the resolution, the bishop of Winchester drew attention to the danger of an Anglican superiority towards the beleaguered churches of the East: "we are apt to put ourselves on a pedestal and to look down upon our brethren." He did not anticipate immediate full communion but looked for a fuller communion. If the Christians of the East appeared to be in a spiritually poor condition this was due to a "want of education."

The draft resolution had spoken of "Orthodox and other Eastern Churches" but the bishop of Salisbury, Dr John Wordsworth, was uneasy that the two should be put together. He wants a clear distinction to be made between the Greek Orthodox and Oriental Orthodox churches. The conference declined to do this and settled for "Eastern Churches" as including both.

The bishop of Aberdeen was afraid that some phrases of the report would wound members of the Orthodox churches — especially the suggestions of reformation. But his plea came too late and was ruled out of order. The bishop of Jerusalem wrote to the archbishop the following day with the conviction that the Orthodox would not take offence. He insisted that Anglicans could not accept re-baptism by the Orthodox.

Half way through the conference an epistle arrived from the Assyrian patriarch to the archbishop of Canterbury (preceded by an advance note from the British consul in Tabriz) and was translated from the Syriac by the dean of Canterbury. The letter was addressed to "his Grace Mar Edward Archbishop of Canterbury and to the Archbishops and Metropolitans and Bishops of the Church of England and to those holding fellowship with her." It began by thanking the archbishop for sending his missionaries (apostles in the original) to the church of the East but then went on to note how much was still to be done to educate his clergy and people. Opposition was noted but there was no explanation of the motives of the "slanderers who weaken the nation worse than its enemies" and who prevent the faithful "having access to the House of God, the words of our Lord, and the Holy Communion." The patriarch rejoiced in the similarities between the Anglican church and the church of the East. He then went on to speak of the lies of those who attributed heresy to the church of the East. He denied those who had slandered the church by alleging: "Lo! in two Christs is her confession, one God and one man separately." The patriarch believed and affirmed that "Lo! the Word became flesh and dwelt in us, and that Christ the Son of God is one in two natures, Divine and Human together in one indivisible Soulhood." The patriarch movingly closed with a repeated request for help for his schools but "still more for your prayers before the throne of mercy that God the Lord of all may enable us to stand and may give us strength in the abundance of His Goodness."

1897

The Lambeth Conference of 1897 passed no special resolutions on the Oriental Orthodox churches. Nor did the committee report on Christian unity deal in any detailed way with these churches. Indeed, some general resistance to closer Anglican-Orthodox relations was registered. The bishop of Cashel argued against spending too much time on Orthodox and Roman Catholic matters (the conference took place only a year after Pope Leo XIII's bull *Apostolicae Curae*). But his speech to the conference revealed that his real attack was as much against Anglo-Catholic eucharistic belief and practice as against Orthodox theology and liturgy.

In spite of this, the churches of the East were discussed first, and Bishop G.F.P. Blyth of Jerusalem reiterated traditional

Anglican policy in the Middle East in terms of ''no aggression to Eastern Churches.'' He went on to speak of Anglican recognition of chrism in the Orthodox and Oriental Orthodox churches as equivalent to confirmation. He also spoke of correspondence with the archbishop of Melbourne, who had written that over 400 Assyrian Christians were without priestly ministration, ''cut off from the rights (sic) of their Church.'' The archbishop of Melbourne had been asked to assist the Assyrian community till a priest could be sent out through the bishop in Jerusalem. The bishop of Salisbury asked how matters had worked out but, enigmatically, there was no time for a formal answer from either the bishop in Jerusalem or the archbishop of Melbourne.

The bishop of Gibraltar spoke about the goal of discussions with the Eastern churches:

> Our Eastern brethren are devotedly attached to their particular Churches and they regard all projects of union with suspicion, fearing they might lead to the disorganization and absorption of their Churches and so to the destruction of their nationality.

He argued for mutual recognition as the goal of Christian unity, with the proper retention of distinctive forms of worship and expressions of faith, government, and ecclesiastical vesture. There should be no ''re-baptism'' or ''re-ordination.''

The bishops then went into committees. The committee which dealt with Christian unity began by dealing with the Eastern churches. A first draft of its report was sent back after the bishop of Worcester accused the committee of glossing over doctrinal differences, especially eucharistic doctrine. As with the bishop of Cashel, contemporary inter-Anglican disputes over Anglo-Catholic teaching appear to be the real cause for this objection.

The bishop of Cairo, Dr Hale, presented a more positive picture of Anglican relations with the Eastern churches. He had been the first Anglican bishop to celebrate the eucharist in the Chapel of Abraham in the Church of the Holy Sepulchre.

During the 1897 conference the bishop of Gibraltar wrote privately to the archbishop of Canterbury (Frederick Temple) proposing a resolution of sympathy with the Armenians in the Ottoman Empire. He sent the archbishop the text of the resolution he was prepared to propose. It spoke in strong terms of "sympathy with our Armenian Brethren in the wrongs and sufferings which they have recently endured," and "our burning indignation at the outrage done to our common humanity by the massacres of which they have been the victims." Perhaps the proposed text was too strong. The archbishop sought the advice of the bishop of Winchester, Randall Davidson. Davidson advised the archbishop against the introduction of such a resolution. He had no objection so long as the conference was unanimous, but this was unlikely, and a public difference of opinion on the matter was worse than no resolution. He also questioned the late introduction of new items onto the agenda. However, as the years and events proceeded, Davidson abandoned this very cautious approach to expressions of solidarity with the Armenians; as archbishop of Canterbury he was later, on more than one occasion, to publicly express Anglican abhorrence at the atrocities inflicted upon the Armenian church and people.

1908

The first bishop to speak on the Oriental Orthodox churches at the 1908 Lambeth Conference was the veteran Bishop Blythe of Jerusalem — this was his third conference. He stressed that Anglican separation from the East did not imply heresy: "severance between the Churches of the West and the East. . . . (is) mainly caused by wars and racial and national quarrels, and not so much by questions of doctrine." He had given informal permission for Anglican priests in his jurisdiction to go as far as to recite the Creed without the *filioque* clause. He proposed a commission to consider reunion and intercommunion with all episcopal churches.

For the first time at a Lambeth conference, the affirmation of an existing unity in faith seriously raised doctrinal issues.

The learned Dr John Wordsworth, the bishop of Salisbury, then made a most important speech. (He was already much interested in the Swedish church and the Old Catholics, and was the drafter of the original Latin *Responsio* of the archbishops of Canterbury and York to Leo XIII's *Apostolicae Curae*.) He went directly to the question of the relation of the Oriental Orthodox churches to the

Council of Chalcedon of 451 which defined Christ in terms of two
"natures," human and divine — terminology unacceptable for
the Oriental Orthodox.

> The separated Churches of the East have never been properly
> treated, if treated at all, by this Conference; they have been
> scarcely noticed as existing; and yet they open a field most
> opportune, I should say, and the most ready of access of any
> field outside the English-speaking races; they are large bodies
> and very kindly disposed bodies. The Armenians number some
> two millions; the Jacobite Syrians have two considerable
> bodies, in Travancore as well as in Syria, and in those regions;
> the Copts number between 700,000 and a million; the Assyrian
> Church, for which I wish specially to plead, has about 100,000
> or 120,000 souls in Assyria, as well as a small branch in Cochin.
> Now inter-communion with all these bodies would be perfectly
> easy, if we could only get over the fact of their formal heresy:
> the heresy in the larger number of cases of Eutychianism,
> attributed to the Jacobites, the Copts and the Armenians, and
> the heresy of Nestorianism attributed to the Assyrians.

The bishop of Salisbury went on to express his view that "the
heresy is formal, rather than real" and urged that the question
should be carefully examined by the committee to be appointed.

The bishop of Moray and Ross, A.J. Maclean, duly presented
the second section of the report of the Conference Reunion Committee. He had experience of the Middle East as a former member
of the staff of the Archbishop's Assyrian Mission. He spoke, as
Wordsworth had requested, of the "separate Churches of the
East, that is to say, bodies which, owing to their not having
accepted the Councils of Ephesus and Chalcedon have, in the
course of history, not by any one act, but in the course of events,
became separate from the life of the rest of the Church." He
stressed that Anglicans had

> no wish or desire to absorb them or make them cease to be
> the ancient Churches which they are. . . . Not only is it an
> important thing that we should endeavour to restore these
> ancient Churches for their own sakes, but also one may con-

fidently hope that in the future they will be able to do what we Westerns cannot do, — they will be able to appeal to the Moslem mind; being Easterns they can speak to Easterns, whereas we Westerns so frequently cannot.

An "awakened" Eastern Christianity as a tool in the evangelization of Muslims was a constant Anglican motivation among those concerned with the church in the Middle East.

The bishop of Moray and Ross spoke of caution over a too rapid advance to intercommunion as there were undoubted doctrinal reasons for their separation from the catholic church. He then proposed that the conference should invite the archbishop of Canterbury to appoint commissions which would investigate the doctrinal questions which still appeared to divide Anglicans from the Oriental Orthodox. He cited that the Armenian and Assyrian churches themselves claimed to be free from Eutychianism or Nestorianism. A commission would be needed to investigate these claims as the conference itself could not adjudicate then and there. As far as the Assyrians were concerned, he conceded that many of their writings used Nestorian language but he also quoted Dr Bright (the distinguished Oxford liturgist) as citing passages from the East Syrian service books which could not possibly have been used by any true Nestorian. He argued that, though they had not accepted the Council of Ephesus, they had informally accepted the Council of Chalcedon. He suggested that the commissions should examine the doctrinal position of the separate Oriental churches and prepare carefully worded statements of faith "as to our Lord's person," in the simplest possible terms, for submission to the churches to ascertain whether the statements accurately represented their faith. He again cited Dr Bright: "your duty . . . is to try and get behind words; try and find out what is really meant by their words and explain to them what we really mean by our words." The commission's findings would be sent to the metropolitans and presiding bishops of all the churches of the Anglican communion.

The bishop of Calcutta concluded by speaking of his diocese, where an explicit agreement had recently been accepted which formalized an existing practice of offering to Armenians emergency baptism and admission to communion where pastoral need required.

The bishop of Moray and Ross then proposed a resolution to put into effect the proposals of the committee. It was accepted overwhelmingly. He then successfully moved a more canonical resolution. Supposing doctrinal agreement were achieved, the resolution proposed mutual admission to communion where the faithful of either tradition were isolated from their own sacraments, and also some provision for occasional communion even where this was not strictly necessary for pastoral reasons but felt to be desirable.

A final resolution was passed on communicating information about any "more formal and complete compact between us and any such Church" to other churches. Here other Chalcedonian churches, especially the Orthodox, were in mind.

These resolutions (Lambeth Conference 1908, nos. 63, 64, and 65) represent a landmark in the formal and doctrinal relations between the churches of the Anglican communion and the Oriental Orthodox churches. (They are appended in full at the end of this section.) This impetus continued its momentum — at least as far as the Syrian and Assyrian churches were concerned — for the archbishop duly appointed a commission which continued the story between the 1908 conference and its successor in 1920 — postponed for two years because of the First World War.

Between 1908 and 1920

In December 1908 the bishop of Salisbury wrote to the archbishop of Canterbury about the implementation of the decisions of the conference. He advised a "general Standing Committee to deal with the separate Churches of the East." He urged an immediate commission to such a committee to deal with the Syrian church because of the presence in England of Patriarch Mar Ignatius Abdullah II. (This was the former Mar Gregorios of Homs, present at the opening of the 1888 conference, who had just published a *Joint Statement of Faith*. A painting of him hangs in Lambeth Palace to this day.) Bishop Wordsworth felt "Providence seems . . . to have marked me out as Chairman for this Eastern Work." He also recommended the appointment of the bishops of Exeter, Ely, Gloucester, Moray and Ross, Gibraltar, Travancore and Cochin, and Jerusalem, together with the assistance of scholars and travellers such as Athelston Riley and W.A. Wigram.

Randall Davidson appointed the bishops and gave them a formal commission to speak with Patriarch Abdullah. John Wordsworth then secured archiepiscopal approval to approach a most distinguished group of consultants, including Swete, Srawley, Brightman, Turner, and Birkbeck.

In July 1910 W.A. Wigram wrote to Davidson about an interview he had had with the Armenian catholicos of Echmiadzin (Ismirlian) while in Tiflis. The catholicos was "not only willing to welcome such intercommunion (as proposed in Resolution 64 of the Conference) but he should be perfectly willing that priests of either communion should, in case of necessity, officiate in the Churches of the other." Wigram invited the archbishop to take this up officially, but Davidson referred it to the new committee under John Wordsworth — as the catholicos was known to be a good man but regarded by fellow Armenians as "something of a Modernist" whose opinions might not be shared by all Armenians.

In the same month Wordsworth reported to Davidson on the progress of the committee. They had decided to put before the Syrian and Assyrian churches, as the "Statement of Faith as to our Lord's Person" requested by the Lambeth Conference, the Christological articles of the *Quicunque Vult* (verses 30-37 of the so-called Athanasian Creed). They also agreed "that at the same time we should (if necessary) ask them to explain in their own terms any expressions in their Creeds or Liturgies which may seem doubtful."

Wordsworth reported interviews with the Syrian patriarch Abdullah. Though the patriarch's disputed position in South India made it very difficult for him to make any authoritative statements of faith, he nevertheless approved the Lambeth Conference resolutions and spoke of the Syrian Creed as authoritative over the whole church — a creed with no trace of monophysitism.

John Wordsworth was anxious to secure real agreement that the union of the two natures in the one person of the Incarnate Christ "took place at the first moment of the Incarnation." He proposed mediating formulations agreed by St Cyril of Alexandria and John of Antioch, and from the seventh-century Nestorian theologian, Babai. The committee were assured that the Assyrian church did not believe in two separate personalities in Christ. But it was nevertheless decided to ask the Assyrian church to explain in what sense it used the term "Mother of Christ, as its technical description of the Blessed Virgin Mary."

The archbishop of Canterbury wrote accordingly to Mar Shimun in July 1910. He received an answer in June 1911. The archbishop's letter had received the approval of all the bishops of the church, and so was as nearly synodical as circumstances allowed. The answer consisted of a full acceptance of the *Quicunque Vult* and a satisfactory explanation of the term *Mother of Christ*.

The commission considered the reply at several sessions in 1911 and 1912, and finally came to the conclusion that the authors of the document had loyally accepted all that the Church of England had proposed as a condition of communion. John Wordsworth died in 1911, but the Committee on the Separated Churches of the East finally wrote to Davidson in April 1912 with their findings on the Assyrian Church of the East. On the basis of the official reply of the catholicos, they declared: "We entertain no doubt that the intention of the document is to profess a bona fide adherence of the Catholic faith concerning the person of our Lord Jesus Christ as set forth in the clauses of the Athanasian Creed." They also accepted the catholicos's statement of faith about the union of the two natures of Christ:

> The Blessed Virgin Mary is the Mother of our Lord and God Jesus Christ, in that from the commencement of the conception of the Humanity of our Lord, God the Word, the second person of the Holy Trinity was united therewith and became one Christ, one Son, in one Person to all eternity.

On this basis the committee declared:

> (This) appears to us to satisfy the conditions of orthodoxy and not to fall short of what we ourselves mean when we use the term *Theotokos* in accordance with the doctrines of the Councils to which we adhere, viz: — Nicaea, Constantinople, Ephesus and Chalcedon.

But to avoid misunderstanding the committee felt it right to point out the ambiguity of Assyrian usage in which the term *Qnuma* was used both of the three "persons" of the Holy Trinity and of the two "natures" of the Incarnate Christ. Because the church of the East was not held to profess the doctrine condemned as Nestorian, the committee did not think it was necessary to demand:

> as a condition of communion that the Assyrian Church should expunge from its Service Books the names of Nestorius and other teachers who have sometimes been anathematized by General Councils, provided that the Assyrian Church for its part, no longer pronounces any censure upon Cyril of Alexandria.

Consequently the committee resolved that action could now be taken as far as the Assyrian church of the East was concerned, and the archbishop was invited to pursue the matter. It was here, perhaps, that John Wordsworth's death was most tragically felt. For no action was taken immediately and the opportunity was allowed to pass. Very soon action became much more difficult owing to the semi-political activities of the Russian Orthodox church. This seemed likely to lead to the submission of the Assyrian church, as the price of political protection. The absence of definite Anglican action, despite warnings from the archbishop's mission personnel, had forced the Assyrians to turn to the Russians. But the outbreak of war put an end to all political and ecclesiastical action.

In 1919 the archbishop of Canterbury — acting on Resolution 61 of the Lambeth Conference of 1908 — established a committee on relations with all the Eastern churches. Bishop Charles Gore was appointed chairman and this committee took over the responsibility of the earlier Committee for the Separated Churches of the East. It immediately resumed the earlier discussions with the Assyrian church by proposing to ask the authorities of the church of the East whether they accepted the declaration made in 1911 by the Assyrian catholicos (who had been killed during the war).

The new committee drafted letters for the archbishop to send to the Assyrian church, but Archbishop Davidson, through his chaplain, George Bell, declined to do this as the present patriarch had just died. His successor, who was appointed in 1920, a boy of 14, was to become a ward of the archbishop of Canterbury and eventually received part of his theological training at St Augustine's College Canterbury.

The Eastern Churches Committee then prepared a memorandum for the forthcoming Lambeth Conference of 1920. The committee, "seeing that opportunity for the establishment of intercommunion may arise at any moment, recommended that the Lambeth Conference should endorse the findings of the earlier Commission in respect to the Assyrian Church." It was suggested that an Assyrian bishop might be present at the conference. It was also recommended that the Lambeth Conference should acknowledge the faithfulness of the Armenian church under persecution and establish "the closest relations" by the "speedy development of mutual intercourse and mutual investigation."

The memorandum also noted the approval of the Armenian authorities in the U.S.A. for Armenians to receive Holy Communion within the Episcopal church when away from their own ministrations (1904). The same thing was happening in India, "with the consent and approval of the Catholicos." Similar provision has been made in the United States for the Syrian Orthodox whose bishop had given permission for the Anglican baptism (to be followed by Syrian chrismation as soon as possible) and marriage of Syrian Orthodox (1910). This permission — it was also noted — had been withdrawn.

1920

It was generally recognized that the First World War had decisively changed the position of all the Eastern churches. The bishop of Kootenay in British Columbia wrote to the archbishop of Canterbury stressing this in the context of a general North American emphasis on the importance of "re-union":

> What effect the war and revolution may have had upon the Eastern Churches by 1920 it is of course impossible to forecast, but undoubtedly they will be facing an absolutely new epoch in their history, and may indeed stand in great need of sympathetic assistance and guidance from our own more favoured Communion.

On the second day of the conference the bishop of Moray and Ross addressed the delegates on the separated churches of the East. He reported on the work of the commission established by the last conference. He spoke of the Assyrians and explained the findings of the committee that the Assyrian language of two *Qnumi* meant two "substances" in the Incarnate Christ, not two "persons." He reminded the conference that "the question is not what Nestorius himself was. The point that we have to decide is whether the East Syrians are really Nestorians."

As far as the (West) Syrian church was concerned, the bishop of Moray reported the 1908 conversations with the Syrian patriarch, Mar Ignatius Abdullah, and denied that the Syrian church was monophysite or patripassian. He then spoke of the "intercommunion between these West Syrians or Jacobites, Armenians, Copts and Abyssinians." He also spoke of the "Christians in Malabar called the Christians of St. Thomas."

Later in the conference the bishop of Moray successfully presented a resolution of sympathy with the Assyrian, Syrian, and Armenian churches. He spoke of their centuries-old endurance of persecution and drew attention to contemporary Kurdish atrocities and the massacre of the Armenians by the Turks. The resolution "deplored with indignation the terrible massacres that have taken place" and called for the establishment of "a righteous government and freedom from oppression for the future."

He then returned to doctrinal matters. He spoke of the unity committee's endorsement of the findings of the post-1908 commission and presented the latter's report to the conference. The conference then passed the following resolution:

> The Conference has received with satisfaction its Committee's Report of the investigations that have been made during the last twelve years with regard to the present doctrinal position of the Separated Churches of the East; and, without expressing an opinion as to the past, believes that these investigations have gone far towards showing that any errors as to the Incarnation of Our Lord which may at some period of their history have been attributed to them, have at any rate now passed away.

The bishop of Moray then turned to the question of intercommunion. This was understood in pastoral terms as occasional eucharistic hospitality. Full visible unity was still the ultimate goal; however, if this were stated immediately, it could be seen as an attempt to proselytize.

The following resolution was enthusiastically carried:

> The Conference repeats the proposal made by the Conference of 1908 that when any of the Separated Churches of the East desire closer relations with us, and wish for the establishment of occasional intercommunion, and give satisfactory assurances as to their faith, such relations should at once be established.

Postscript

The period 1908-1920 is clearly a high-water mark in Anglican-Oriental Orthodox relations. However, for a variety of reasons, impetus was then lost on both sides. Perhaps only now is the momentum being regained through direct contacts with the individual Oriental Orthodox churches and through the Anglican Oriental Orthodox Forum. As Anglicans seek to break fresh ground in their relations with the Oriental Orthodox, it will be as well to learn both positive and negative lessons from the early Lambeth Conferences.

From 1878-1920 certain constant features run through the Lambeth fathers' discussions about the "Separate Churches of the East." A pastoral duty of solicitude and solidarity is recognized; the Oriental Orthodox are seen to be brothers and sisters in Christ, whose churches originated in the heartlands of original Christianity and whose adherents have suffered grievously for their faith in Christ, both in the past and in the contemporary world. Along with this pastoral duty comes a frank recognition that one motive in the desire of the Oriental Orthodox for closer relations with Anglicans was the possible protection this might have afforded persecuted Christian minorities in the political confusions of the demise of the Ottoman Empire. While the Lambeth fathers seem to have accepted this as perfectly proper, very little appears to have been said or done until the enormities of the genocide of the Armenians came to public knowledge in the early twenties.

Another constant is the firm and declared policy of no proselytization. In this Anglicans have an honourable record which has engendered trust and affection. There was a constant recognition that premature talk about unity or union would be perceived as interference with the structures and traditions of ancient autonomous churches — a problem the Oriental churches experienced in different ways from both Roman Catholic and Protestant missions at that time. Mutual eucharistic hospitality and pastoral care were seen as the immediate goal, and it came within a hair's breadth of achievement.

As far as doctrine was concerned, the early Lambeth Conferences clearly wanted to give the Oriental churches the benefit of the doubt without in any way abandoning Chalcedonian orthodoxy. There was clear recognition that the substance of the faith might be expressed in more than one way and in various compatible terms.

A clear theological distinction was also drawn between the Oriental churches proper and the Assyrian Church of the East.

Lambeth 1920 was a point of departure. But there was no systematic implementation of the proposals worked out between 1908 and 1920. The disruption of war, the dissolution of empire, and the wholesale migration of peoples made communication more and more difficult. Meanwhile, on the Anglican side, other ecumenical interests began to displace the earlier emphasis on the Oriental churches: Constantinople, the Swedish Lutheran church, "Home Reunion," South India, the Old Catholics, and even Rome.

A partial exception is the Syrian Orthodox church. In 1922 Patriarch Mar Ignatius Elias III was in correspondence with the Eastern Churches Committee. It had enquired on what conditions Syrian Orthodox, resident in the West (especially in America), could receive sacramental ministrations from Anglican clergy when unable to receive the ministrations of their own church. The patriarch was able to reassure the committee on essential points of Christology. This included an affirmation of the key Chalcedonian phrase on the unity between the divinity and humanity of the "One Indivisible Christ": "a union without confusion, change, division, mixture, transformation or separation."

Accordingly, Archbishop Davidson wrote to him in terms of the 1908 and 1920 Lambeth Conferences, authorizing members of the Syrian church for admission to Holy Communion, Baptism, and marriage both when away from their own churches and even in special cases when this was not the case. The archbishop invited the patriarch to suggest any special procedures to be observed when Syrian Orthodox availed themselves of this permission. Late in the same year, the patriarch thanked the archbishop, noting only that Syrian Orthodox should make a confession of sin "according to the rules of the Church" before receiving Holy Communion. But he added significantly that he could not "proclaim this arrangement" before a meeting of the "Council of our Metropolitans and Bishops" and "the meeting of this Council is not possible, because the Metropolitans and Bishops belong to different governments." He added poignantly, "my hope is that when peace comes in the Near East I may ask them to meet me, to study the question of union." As with the Assyrians a decade before, synodical endorsement of agreement was impossible for political reasons.

Succeeding Lambeth Conferences could do no more than note this state of affairs. With Armenians the situation was hardly better, though there was valuable conversation with Bishop Tourian the Armenian observer at the 1930 conference. At the 1948 conference hopes were expressed for discussions with the Armenian Orthodox but these were unfulfilled. At the same time good relations were noted with the Coptic and Ethiopian Orthodox churches. 1958 reported "little to record in the way of advance in official contacts since 1948." 1968 noted the inter-Oriental Orthodox Conference at Addis Ababa of 1965 and hoped that there might be a fruitful dialogue. 1978 said nothing at all.

However, developments, recorded elsewhere in this volume, have occurred since then. These encourage hope for a growth in formal relations between Anglicans and Oriental Orthodox to match the warm personal relations which have existed ever since contacts between the two groups began in the early nineteenth century. I hope this chapter will show just how far those formal relations had come with some of the Oriental churches, and will give Anglicans and Oriental Orthodox some inspiration to continue the work of the pioneers.

Note

The bulk of this chapter has been taken from the minutes and correspondence of the Lambeth Conferences and the Douglas Papers, both in the Lambeth Palace Library. The reports and resolutions of the Lambeth Conferences are accessible in various editions published (up to 1968) by SPCK. For convenience the key resolutions of 1908 are included here.

63. The Conference would welcome any steps that might be taken to ascertain the precise doctrinal position of the ancient separate Churches of the East with a view to possible inter-communion, and would suggest to the Archbishop of Canterbury the appointment of Commissions to examine the doctrinal position of particular Churches, and (for example) to prepare some carefully framed statement of the Faith as to our Lord's Person, in the simplest possible terms, which should be submitted to each of such Churches, where feasible, in order to ascertain whether it represents their belief with substantial accuracy. The conclusions of such Commissions should in our opinion be submitted to the Metropolitans or Presiding Bishops of all the Churches of the Anglican Communion.

64. In the event of doctrinal agreement being reached with such separate Churches, the Conference is of opinion that it would be right (1) for any Church of the Anglican Communion to admit individual communicant members of those Churches to communicate with us when they are deprived of this means of grace through isolation, and conversely, for our communicants to seek the same privileges in similar circumstances; (2) for the Churches of the Anglican Communion to permit our communicants to communicate on special occasions with these Churches, even when not deprived of this means of grace through isolation, and conversely, that their communicants should be allowed the same privileges in similar circumstances.

65. We consider that any more formal and complete compact between us and any such Church, seeing that it might affect our relations with certain other Churches, should not take place without previous communication with any other Church which might be affected thereby.

Conclusion

Henry Hill

One must admit the impossibility of a total analysis of the conditions of the ancient churches in South India and the Middle East; however, we believe the chapters which have preceded will have given readers some well-informed insights.

Perhaps an illustration of the general situation that these churches find themselves in today can be drawn from a conversation which took place in August 1986 between His Holiness Karekin II, the Armenian catholicos of Cilicia (Lebanon), and several Canadian ecumenists. The catholicos remarked that although some would advocate the withdrawal of the indigenous churches from their ancient homelands (e.g., Lebanon, Iraq, and Iran) to other parts of the world, he personally felt this would be a false solution. The Armenians, with the other Eastern and Oriental Orthodox churches, have endured holocausts and persecutions which were far worse than those of the present day. The catholicos went on to say that we must draw a distinction between the conditions of warfare, the violent outbursts, car bombings, and kidnappings, etc., and the daily lives of ordinary people who are trying to maintain some degree of normalcy.

The Western churches need to remember that the Middle East is the cradle of Christianity and to see their responsibilities in this light. This message was given by the archbishop of Canterbury in his address at the conclusion of the Anglican Oriental Orthodox Forum in Canterbury on 10 October 1985. No church ought to take part in the missionary activities of a former age; the responsibility of our time is to lend support to the ancient churches for the task which God has given *them* to do. Our support of *their* churches, clinics, hospitals, schools, and welfare institutions is a necessary one, particularly in Lebanon where the churches must provide for their own people. Our communion of love is of vital importance.

Christians are called to participate in the reality of the Incarnation which is the central fact of our faith. "The Word became flesh, and dwelt among us" (Jn 1:14); living, dying, and rising in our humanity, he has taken us with him to the Father in the life of the Holy Spirit. As Matthew the Poor put it, "This truth (the eternal Sonship of Christ to God) Christ firmly established in the minds of His disciples so that all would perceive in it the mystery of His personal relationship to the Father, a mystery that would be in itself a medium drawing us closer *in Him* to God as a Father of ours as well" (Father Matthew the Poor).

While we must maintain the true faith of Christ's humanity and divinity in one person, we dare not indulge in the debates which divided Christendom in the earlier centuries of our history. "Have you come," asked an Oriental Orthodox bishop of two Anglican visitors, "to talk about the old controversies? If you have, we shall discuss them with you; but we shall go around in circles and get nowhere! Have you come to help us solve our problems? You cannot solve them, nor can we solve yours; but if you have come in friendship, then perhaps we can learn to trust one another, and to share those things which are most important to us; our prayer and our Faith in action."

Before the Catholicos Karekin II left Lebanon in August 1986, he went as in duty-bound to visit the president of his country who asked him to deliver a message to Canada and the United States; that is to look no longer at the political but at the human and the social situation.

The tragedy is that so many see disasters only from the perspective of this world. "We can only stand before some of these and wring our hands" (a saying of Archbishop Ted Scott, former primate of the Anglican Church of Canada), but we must do what we can. Many of us have no first-hand experience of the society in which our sister churches live, but we have the presence of the diaspora in many English-speaking countries, not least of all in Australia, Canada, Great Britain, and the United States. A starting point can be to reach out to them from where we are. It is one thing to know something about their churches; it is quite another to know them at first hand. One contact leads to another, and many have made contact before us. In this way, in knowledge and friendship, we may be enabled to stand alongside one another.

Here, then, are a few brief suggestions as to where we can locate their communities.

The Armenian Church

His Holiness Vasken I, patriarch catholicos of all 3,350,626 member Armenians, lives in Echmiadzin, U.S.S.R. His Holiness has immediate jurisdiction over Soviet Armenia and the U.S.S.R., including Iran, Iraq, India, Egypt, Ethiopia, Europe, and the Americas. The ancient sees under the aegis of holy Echmiadzin are the patriarchate of Jerusalem, which is centred at St James Monastery in Jerusalem and is responsible for the holy places which belong to the Armenian church (the present occupant of the see is His Beatitude Yegishe Derderian, P.O. Box 14001, Jerusalem, Israel); and the patriarchate of Constantinople with jurisdiction over all Armenian Orthodox in Turkey (the patriarch is His Beatitude Schnork Kalustian, Kumpapi, Ermeni Patriklig, Sarapnel Sokak, TR-34480, Istanbul, Turkey.

The Canadian primate, Bishop Vasken Keshishian, began his episcopate in 1984 and has his headquarters at St Gregory the Illuminator Cathedral, 615 Rue Stuart, Outremont, Quebec H2V 3H2; the parish is well organized and has a large parochial school.

In Toronto there is Holy Trinity Church, 14 Woodlawn Avenue. The parish is so named because it began in Holy Trinity (Anglican) Church, Eaton Square, under the patronage of the Most Reverend Derwyn Owen, archbishop of Toronto. The congregation has built a large, new parish church, consecrated by H.H. Vasken I, October 1987. The pastor is the Very Reverend Hovnan Derderian (Tel. 416-924-6514).

Other parishes in Canada are: St Gregory the Illuminator, St Catharine's, Ontario; St Mary, Hamilton, Ontario; and St Vartan, Vancouver, British Columbia.

The diocese publishes *Abaka*, a weekly journal in Armenian, English, and French.

The Eastern diocese of the Armenian Church of America has

its headquarters at: 630 Second Avenue, New York, NY 10016 (Tel. 212-686-0710). The primate is Archbishop Torkom Manoogian. St Vartan Cathedral in New York was consecrated in 1968 by His Holiness Vasken I.

The western diocese of California was formed under its own primate in 1928, and is now under Bishop Vatche Hovsepian, 4511 Orchid Drive, Los Angeles, CA 90043 (Tel. 213-466-5266).

The Armenian Church of America is located largely along the eastern seaboard, in greater Detroit, Chicago, and California; in sixty-five parishes ministering to 500,000 communicants in Canada and the U.S.A. The church has its own seminary in the United States, although some clergy have studied at the General Seminary in New York, and at Trinity College, Toronto. The church publishes two periodicals, *Bema*, a monthly, mostly English for the eastern diocese; and *Mother Church*, also monthly, for the western diocese. For further information in the United States contact, the Reverend Father Arten Ashjian, 630 Second Avenue, New York, NY 10016.

The United Kingdom is under the Right Reverend Bishop Yegishe Gizirian, c/o the Armenian Vicarage, Iverna Gardens, London, W8 6TP (Tel. 01 937 0152).

The catholicosate of Cilicia is a parallel jurisdiction of the Armenian Apostolic Church in Canada and the U.S.A. under His Holiness Karekin II, catholicos of Cilicia, Antelias, Beirut, Lebanon. Differences between the supreme catholicosate in Echmiadzin and the catholicosate of Cilicia are being negotiated.

Canadian parishes under the jurisdiction of Cilicia are as follows. St Mary's parish in Toronto meets at present in the Anglican church of St Augustine of Canterbury on Bayview Avenue, but is also in the process of building a permanent church of its own. Its pastor is the Very Reverend Father Khajog Hagopian (Tel. 416-403-8122). The parish of St. Gregory the Illuminator is in Cambridge, Ontario.

In Montreal St James (Sourp Hagop) is a flourishing parish with a large parochial school; 3041 Olivier Asselin, Montreal, Quebec. The pastor is the Very Reverend Armen Ishkhanian.

St Mary's parish has recently been established in Vancouver. It's mailing address is P.O. Box 58386, Station "C", Vancouver, British Columbia V6P 6E4 (Tel. 604-946-8245).

The church in the U.S.A. is larger than in Canada and has epis-
copal oversight of both countries. Bishop Mesrob Ashdjian of
New York is the primate of Eastern U.S.A. and Canada, at 138
East 39th Street, New York, NY 10016 (Tel. 212-689-7810).

Archbishop Datev Sarkissian of Los Angeles is the primate of
Western U.S.A. and Canada; c/o Armenian Prelacy, 4401 Russell
Avenue, Los Angeles, CA 90027 (Tel. 213-663-8273). Until 1985
the archbishop was dean of the Theological Seminary at Bikfaya,
Lebanon. He was also a member of the Anglican Oriental Ortho-
dox Theological Forum in 1985.

The Coptic Church

The Coptic Orthodox church is led by Pope Shenouda III, Pope
of Alexandria, Cairo, Egypt.

The first Canadian parish of St Mark's, 4 Glendinning Ave.,
Scarborough was organized in Toronto by Father Marcos Marcos
in 1965. As the story goes, the Anglican Sisters of St John the
Divine advertised the sale of an altar screen. Father Marcos
answered the advertisement. When asked, the Reverend Mother
said, ''There will be a price.'' ''Of course,'' said Father Marcos,
''how much?'' ''That you pray for us at every service,'' was the
reply. ''And'' says Father Marcos, ''we have always done so.''
What he does not say was that the church was built to fit the
screen! There are two other parishes in southern Ontario; the
Church of St Mary the Virgin and St Athanasius, 1245 Eglinton
Ave. W., Mississauga, and the Church of St Mary, 50 Augusta
Street, Cambridge, Ontario. There are two churches in Montreal
and one, St Mary and St Mark, in Edmonton.

Holiness the Pope as its immediate bishop. The first U.S. parish
was established in 1970 by Father Gabriel Abdelsayed in New
York and New Jersey. Present diocesan headquarters are St Mark
in Toronto (for Canada) and St Mark in New Jersey (for the United
States). There are roughly 150,000 communicants in the United
States and 50,000 in Canada. There are twenty-five ordained
priests in the United States and six in Canada. Each parish church
has its own periodical, published mainly in English and Arabic.

For further information in Canada contact: The Very Reverend
Father Marcos Marcos, 107 Placentia Boulevard, Scarborough,

Ontario M1S 4C9 (Tel. 416-298-3355). In the U.S.A. contact: the Very Reverend Dr Gabriel A. Abdelsayed, 429 West Side Avenue, Jersey City, NJ 07304.

In England contact: the Coptic Orthodox church, the Reverend Father Bishoy Boushra, 29 Palace Mansions, Earsby Street, London W14 89W (Tel. 01 603 6701); The Reverend Father Antonius Faraq, 36 Warwick Chambers, Peter Street, London W8 (Tel. 01 937 0367); The Reverend Father Antonius Sabet, 14 Newton Mansion, Queens Club Gardens, London W14 (Tel. 01 385 1991—home, 01 937 5782 church).

The Ethiopian Orthodox Church

The Ethiopian Orthodox church is under the leadership of His Holiness Tekle Haimanot, Patriarch of Ethiopia.

The diocese of the Western hemisphere was established in 1972. His Eminence Abuna Yesehaq is its archbishop, assisted by an auxiliary bishop in the United States. The present diocesan headquarters are located at 140-142 West 176th Street, Bronx, NY 10453.

In Toronto the first Ethiopian parish opened in a tiny storefront at 425 Vaughan Road on Palm Sunday (Hosannah), 27 April 1986. Its permanent priest is the Reverend L.K. Messale Engeda. The preacher on the occasion was Bishop Henry Hill. It is a congregation composed largely of Ethiopians and some Jamaican Rastifarians. There are 5,000 Ethiopians in Toronto.

There is a parish in London, England; the Very Reverend Archimandrite Aragwi Wolde Gabriel, 253 Ladbroke Grove, London W10 (Tel 01 249 0221).

Other Ethiopian communities are found in California, England, Bermuda, Guyana, Jamaica, Trinidad and Tobago, and St Kitts (West Indies).

There are in all the churches of the Western hemisphere about 90,000 communicants, comprising both Western-born and Ethiopians. There are forty-one ordained priests in the diocese.

A Handbook of the Ethiopian Orthodox Church has been prepared by the Reverend L.K. Messale Engeda and was published by the Anglican Book Centre, Toronto, with financial assistance from the Anglican Church of Canada.

The Syrian Orthodox Church

The Syrian Orthodox church in North America is under His Holiness Ignatius Sakka Ivas, patriarch of Antiochia and All the East, Damascus, Syria.

The primate of the Syrian Orthodox in Canada and the United States is Mar Athanasios Yeshue Samuel, 49 Kipp Avenue, Lodi, NJ 07644 (Tel 201-778-0638).

There are four parishes in Canada: St Barsaumo, 72 Birchmount Road, Scarborough (Toronto), Ontario; St Mark, 1202 Dunsmure Road, Hamilton, Ontario; St Jacques, 750 St Joseph Boulevard East, Montreal, Quebec; St Ephrem, 130 13th Avenue S., Sherbrooke, Quebec. There are eight parishes in the United States; two in New Jersey, one in Rhode Island, one in Boston, one in Worcester, Massachusetts, one in Chicago, one in Detroit, one in Los Angeles.

The presence of Syrian Orthodox in North America dates back to the late nineteenth century when faithful started to emigrate from Turkey to the United States and Canada. Syrian faithful from Diyarbekir, Turkey, qualified as silk workers, settled in New Jersey, a major area of the silk industry. Families from Harput, Turkey, were drawn to Massachusetts, while faithful from the Turkish province of Tur'Abdin, being chiefly weavers by trade, established themselves in Rhode Island as employees in the local weaving mills. (Families from Mardin, Turkey, were to settle in the province of Quebec during the same period.) Meanwhile, Syrian Orthodox from villages near Homs, Syria, journeyed to the United States to settle in and around Detroit, Michigan.

The archdiocese currently numbers approximately 30,000 communicants, and is presently served by twenty-three priests, with two retired pastors. For further information contact: His Eminence Archbishop Mar Athanasius Yeshue Samuel, the Very Reverend Chorepiscopus John Meno, Archdiocesan General Secretary, 45 Fairmount Avenue, Hackensack, NJ 07601.

The two Syrian Orthodox centres in Europe are St Aphrem Syrian Orthodox Cathedral in Stockholm and St Ephrem monastery in Losser, the Netherlands.

The Syrian Orthodox Church of Antioch in India also has a number of congregations in the United States. In England (temporary) the contact is Metropolitan Timotheus Aphrem Aboodi, 2 Whitecroft Way, Beckenham, Kent (Tel. 650 3837)

The Syrian Orthodox Church in India, independent of Antioch, is under His Holiness Moran Mar Baselius Mar Thoma I Mathews in Kottayam, Kerala, India.

For the United States the contact is His Grace Thomas Mar Makarios, Metropolitan of the Americas, Episcopal Diocesan House, 1114 Delaware Avenue, Buffalo, NY 14209 (Tel. 415-548-2202).

In Canada a group of Syrian Orthodox meet at Trinity College, Toronto, at 11:00 a.m., the first Sunday of the month. There are also congregations in Kingston and Ottawa.

In England there is a congregation led by the Reverend K.A. George, 154 Bramley Road, London N14 4HU (Tel. 01 449 2915).

In India there are about one and a half million faithful in each of the two churches. Hope still exists for their eventual reconciliation. Both jurisdictions participated in the Anglican Oriental Orthodox Forum at St Albans in 1985.

The Assyrian Church of the East

Today the Catholicos Patriarch Mar Dinkha IV has his patriarchal cell at 8908 Birch Avenue Morton Grove, Il 60053. There are churches in London. There are also dioceses in Iraq, Iran, Syria, Lebanon, Italy, and South India:

Mar Slewa Gewargis, metropolitan of Iraq.

Mar Yousif Sargis, bishop for the diocese of Baghdad, Iraq.

Mar Daniel Yacoub, bishop of Kirkuk, Iraq.

Mar Narsi Elias De Baz, metropolitan of Lebanon and Europe.

Mar Aprim Khamis, bishop for the diocese of Eastern United States and Canada.

Mar Ashur Bawai, bishop for the diocese of Western United States.

Mar Meelis Zia, bishop for the diocese of Australia.

Mar Claudio Vittorozo, bishop for the diocese of Aqualia, Italy.

The diocese of Iran — vacant.

The diocese of Syria — vacant — His Beatitude Bishop Mar Youkhana Ibrahim died in 1986. His representative in England is the Very Reverend Yonan Yonan, 89 Leighton Road, West Ealing, London W13.

Postscript

It is the quest of all Christians to become more aware of the workings of the Holy Spirit, not only in their own communions but in others sometimes little known to them, for we are living parts of the One Holy Catholic and Apostolic Church. This is the voyage of discovery, marked by the presence of Christ in our midst.

It is the hope of the authors of this book that the information conveyed will, under the influence of the same Holy Spirit, be given some practical application by those who read it.

"Unity is the fusion of the one into the other, to put an end to the many; therefore, in outward appearance unity is weakness, but in essence it is an immense force, as indivisible as God" (Father Matthew the Poor).

Sources

The Oriental Orthodox Churches in the United States. Secretariat, Bishops' Committee for Ecumenical and Interreligious Affairs, National Conference of Catholic Bishops.
Orthodoxia 1986-1987, OSC Kirchuches Institut, Regensburg.
Roberson, Ronald G., CSP, *The Eastern Churches, A Brief Survey.* Roma: Paulist Press, 1986.